AF333097

WHAT OTHERS ARE SAYING

When I first became acquainted with Marilyn Tyner, I was impressed with her passion for Jesus, her grasp of apologetics, and her love for God's Word. At that time Marilyn had just begun writing pamphlets that succinctly captured the basic doctrines of the Bible in an accessible way. Her tracts were a tremendous asset to me in ministry and working with Bible college students. As I recently read through her devotional book, *Awesom-azing God*, not only was I blessed and encouraged, but I recognized Marilyn's giftedness in her ability to passionately describe the great attributes of our amazing Lord. This devotional will excite, inspire, and undergird your faith as you peruse the awesome and amazing virtues of our God!

—Cheryl Brodersen,
Author, conference speaker, TV and radio host,
head pastor's wife, Calvary Chapel Costa Mesa

If you want to be captivated by the living and true God in a personal, engaging, and exciting way, this is the book for you! It is a soul-satisfying study of the characteristics of the biblical God. Given that A. W. Tozer said, "What you think of God is the most important thing about you" (*Knowledge of the Holy*), this could be one of the most important books you ever read.

—Dr. Norman L. Geisler,
Chancellor and Distinguished Professor of Apologetics
and Theology, Veritas Evangelical Seminary,
Costa Mesa, California

Through personal and powerful devotionals, *Awesomazing God* showcases the true and living God and His attributes. Believers will be enriched in their relationship with Him and more inspired to live for His glory. The apologetics interspersed in the book will equip readers to share Jesus Christ in today's spiritually mixed-up world. Marilyn Tyner's work as an apologist is thorough and well thought out.

—Carl Westerlund,
Director
Calvary Chapel Bible College Graduate School

Your heart will be encouraged, your faith will be strengthened, and your desire to share the gospel will be intensified as you meditate on the immutable attributes of God as brilliantly presented in this book. This timely devotion will ignite your passion to not only know our "Awesomazing God" better but also to passionately share Him with everyone you meet!

—Kathy Morales, Ed.D.
Dean of Women
Calvary Chapel University

Marilyn Tyner is a rare asset in the evangelical church today. She knows her way around Scripture, is deeply devoted to God, and knows how to persuasively answer objections to faith in Christ. I have been a fan of her wonderfully written gospel tracts and was delighted to hear she was writing a devotional book. After reading through it, my delight was justified. Not only is it thoughtful and moving, but it is very well written. It will be perfect for personal devotions and very effective for group studies. Marilyn has done it again!

—Craig J. Hazen, PhD
Founder and Director
Christian Apologetics Graduate Program
Biola University, La Mirada, California

A gifted apologist and author, Marilyn Tyner serves up a meaty, satisfying meal with delicious sauces drawn from experience—anecdotes from her own life, the lives of friends, other writers, and people in Scripture—all perfectly chosen to complement each course. She makes rich theological truths readable and imbues them with warmth, sharing herself with a transparency that draws us to her…and through her to the One she invites us to know more intimately.

Until I read *Awesom-azing God*, I didn't realize how much I have been missing the deep truths of the Word of God. Marilyn expresses them in a way that leads the reader right into the throne room of our living Lord to worship Him in all His majesty. There is an awe and reverence here that I don't often see in Christian writing. This book will bring you back to your first love, to the delight of knowing and worshipping Him in all His awesom-azing facets.

—Jessica Shaver Renshaw,
Journalist and Author
Gianna: Aborted…and Lived to Tell About It, Tyndale House

This unique devotional magnifies God and His attributes by blending scriptural teachings, personal stories, and apologetics. Marilyn Tyner's book establishes that God is not just awesom-azing because Christians believe great things about Him, but because He is the true and living God! He's the One who declared, "Let him who glories glory in this, that he understands and knows Me, that I am the Lord" (Jer. 9:24). Readers will surely come to know Him better and be drawn into a deeper devotional life.

—Larry DiSimone,
Pastor and Apologist
Calvary Chapel of the Canyons,
Silverado Canyon, California

Marilyn Tyner has produced a remarkable book of great substance and powerful teaching. She is deeply grounded in Scripture and adept at translating this into useful apologetics. And this is vital—because if we don't know the God of the Bible, we will likely create Him in our image. But this is more than a solid teaching book. It's also a collection of true stories, by real people, about a God who is accessible to us. The Spirit of God will take her words in black-and-white print and turn them into spirit and life that will touch you deeply. I heartily recommend this book!

——Susan D. Hill,
Author, *Closer Than Your Skin: Unwrapping the Mystery of Intimacy with God*, WaterBrook Press

Awesom-azing God is sure to encourage new believers, as well as seasoned Christians, with Marilyn's knowledge of apologetics. We use her True-Way Tracts at our international outreach locations through "Lighting the Way Worldwide" and often hear people say they want to have Bible studies and Sunday school classes based on Marilyn's teachings. This devotional will bless the daily walk of any Christian.

—Dwayna Litz,
Founder
Lighting the Way Worldwide

I whole-heartedly recommend this book! In *Awesom-azing God*, Marilyn writes that "the simplest definition of Christianity is knowing God," and she helps you do exactly that. You will find that she carefully explores God's attributes by combining biblical truth, history, apologetics, and personal testimony, as well amusing anecdotes that make you smile as you wade through the deep theological waters this book offers. Get out your forks and knives, Christians, as it's time to dine on some meat!

—Sarah Ankenman,
Director
International Society of Women in Apologetics

AWESOM-AZING GOD

Awesom-azing God

KNOW HIM
LOVE HIM
PROCLAIM HIM

Marilyn Joy Tyner

TATE PUBLISHING
AND ENTERPRISES, LLC

Awesom-azing God
Copyright © 2015 by Marilyn Joy Tyner. All rights reserved.

No part of this publication may be reproduced, stored in a retrieval system, or transmitted in any way by any means, electronic, mechanical, photocopy, recording, or otherwise without the prior permission of the author except as provided by USA copyright law.

Unless otherwise indicated, all Scripture quotations in this publication are from the *New King James Version*. Copyright ©1982 by Thomas Nelson, Inc. Used by permission. All rights reserved.

Scripture quotations marked (NLT) are taken from the *Holy Bible, New Living Translation*, copyright ©1996, 2004, 2007 by Tyndale House Publishers, Inc., Carol Stream, Illinois 60188. All rights reserved.

Scripture quotations marked (AMP) are taken from the Amplified® Bible, Copyright © 1954, 1958, 1962, 1964, 1965, 1987 by The Lockman Foundation. Used by permission.

The opinions expressed by the author are not necessarily those of Tate Publishing, LLC.

Published by Tate Publishing & Enterprises, LLC
127 E. Trade Center Terrace | Mustang, Oklahoma 73064 USA
1.888.361.9473 | www.tatepublishing.com

Tate Publishing is committed to excellence in the publishing industry. The company reflects the philosophy established by the founders, based on Psalm 68:11,
"The Lord gave the word and great was the company of those who published it."

Book design copyright © 2015 by Tate Publishing, LLC. All rights reserved.
Cover design by Rtor Maghuyop
Interior design by Jimmy Sevilleno

Published in the United States of America

ISBN: 978-1-63449-252-2
1. Religion / Christian Life / Devotional
2. Religion / Christian Theology / Apologetics
15.02.24

To my beloved husband and prayer partner, Tom.

And to my two wonderful sons, Donovan and Tony,
and their family members:
Bobbi, Cayla, Timmee.
Linda, Kortney, Jenna, Nicky.

Also to my beloved "acquired" family members:
Debbie, Barry, Jake, Cole.
Keith, Debbie, Keith Jr., Jeremy, Tommy, Brooke,
Aaron, Ashley, McKenna, Logan, Rylee, Summer, Ella.
Carrie, Roy, Russell, Cheylene.
Sherry, Benny, Nicole, Dylan, Gage.
Lori, Mike, Dustin, Brandon, Joey.

*Seek first the kingdom of God and His righteousness,
and all these things shall be added to you.
(Matt. 6:33)*

CONTENTS

FOREWORD

There has never been a better time to remind ourselves of who and what God is. A. W. Tozer lived in a similar spiritual climate in the mid-twentieth century, when Christians were in jeopardy of losing touch with the orthodox nature of God. To address this alarming trend, he penned his short treatise *Knowledge of the Holy*, which focused on the glorious attributes of the Holy One. Marilyn Tyner's *Awesom-azing God* serves the same high purpose today—with a unique devotional approach.

As I read this devotional book, I was impressed not only by the rich doctrinal content but by the cogent and concise apologetic emphasis interwoven throughout its chapters. The author acknowledges the crucial relationship between *what* Christians believe and *why* they believe it, and she seeks to close the gap in our knowledge between the two domains.

Marilyn Tyner recognizes the importance of both doctrinal integrity and personal devotion to our Creator. Her education, ministry experience, and clear and creative writing style have placed God's attributes under the microscope for the world to see. These insightful devotionals anchor readers in the truth while preparing their hearts and minds to defend the faith. Each chapter is innovative and smart, offering much-needed refreshment and education to the spiritually hungry.

Marilyn has made it easy, convenient, and rewarding to get into the Word. As she unpacks each of the glorious titles and descriptions of God, you will find yourself being drawn into a closer relationship with Christ, and you will come to know Him like never before.

—Joseph M. Holden, PhD
President, Veritas Evangelical Seminary

INTRODUCTION

GOD IS BEYOND AWESOME, BEYOND AMAZING

DESPITE COMPETING VOICES in our spiritually mixed-up world, the living God who reveals Himself in the Bible reigns. And nothing can compare to walking through life in fellowship with Him through His Son, Jesus Christ. Yet many believers have only a hazy concept of who God is and have a difficult time explaining Him to others. If we truly desire to "hallow" His name—as we recite in the Lord's Prayer in Luke 11—we need to know who He is.[1]

Mary of Bethany delighted in getting to know Jesus Christ more deeply. She spent time sitting at His feet, adoring Him and listening to His words of truth and grace (Luke 10:39). As a result, Jesus made an astounding statement: "One thing is needed, and Mary has chosen that good part, which will not be taken away from her" (v. 42). What was that "one needed thing"? A continual focus on Jesus.

This book is designed to help you enjoy that *one thing* more than ever. As you marvel at God's awesom-azing attributes, you will find yourself engaging with Jesus in more loving fellowship. You will also be inspired to use your spiritual giftings to advance the gospel and God's kingdom. For to know Him is to love Him, and to love Him is to naturally share who He is with others.

While people are free to call on lesser gods of their own choosing, someday unbelievers will discover what they missed by not responding to their loving and merciful Creator (Gen. 1:1) and preparing themselves for eternal concerns (Matt. 25:21; 2 Peter 1:11).

GOD'S AWESOM-AZING ATTRIBUTES

This book showcases diamond-like facets of our multi-faceted Lord. If you meditate on them, you will come to trust Him more completely, embrace Him more dearly, worship Him more genuinely, respond to Him with more humility and obedience, gain a greater awareness of His presence, and reflect His radiance to others.

Dr. Norman Geisler, a prominent theologian and the author of *Systematic Theology in One Volume*, writes this about the importance of studying God's attributes:

> Few, if any, studies are more important than that of the attributes of God. There are many reasons for this, including: All basic theological truth depends upon God's attributes; we cannot recognize false "gods" without knowing the true God; our spiritual growth is dependent upon our concept of God; the desire for infinite happiness cannot be found in anything short of the Infinite God. . . . Contemplating the Creator should change the creature; meditating on the Master should make a difference in the life of the servant.[2]

We will focus on God's attributes through a collection of ninety-nine devotions, comprised of Bible snapshots and personal stories.

Ten Glorious Titles of God

The chapter titles present ten names for God, which align with the twenty-five classic attributes of God revealed in the Bible, as listed below. (For definitions of these terms, see Appendix A.) The chapter subtitles highlight wondrous ways in which our Lord personally relates to us as His sons and daughters.

The Fountain of Living Water
Quenches our spiritual thirst
He is holy, and He is life (and the source of all life).
Our Matchless King
Treats us as His royal sons and daughters
He is sovereign, and He is/has majesty and eternality.
The God Who's There
Dwells within us and never leaves
He is omnipresent, and He is immutable.
Our Divine Sympathizer
Ministers to our deepest needs
He is omnibenevolent (all love/goodness), and He is omnipotent.
The Light of the World
Reveals Himself to us personally
He is light, He is beauty, and He is transcendent.
Our Royal Redeemer
Rescues us and brings us victories
He is righteous (just), and He is/has wisdom.
The Treasured Trinity
Reveals His transcendent love for us
He is triune within His unity, and He is/has immortality.
The God of All Truth
Blesses us with genuine truth
He is omniscient, and He is/has immateriality and truthfulness.
Our Priceless Pathway
Invites us to walk with Him

He is jealous, and He is/has moral perfection.

The Everlasting God
Offers us eternal life with Him
He is infinite, He is ineffable, and He is/has impassibility.[3]

AN APOLOGETICS EMPHASIS

A special feature of this book is its presentation of twenty-one text boxes of apologetics, which present top evidences for the truth of Christianity. They will prepare you to confidently answer questions posed by skeptics and searchers. Then you can transition your conversations to the subject of our Savior and His mission. After all, the God of the Bible is awesom-azing not just because Christians believe it, but because there is compelling evidence that demonstrates He is the true and living God.

- Religion vs. Relationship
- Which Religion Is the Oldest?
- The Messianic Line Preserved
- Fulfilled Messianic Prophecies
- Pascal's Wager: An Appeal to Atheists
- God's Supreme Revelation of Himself
- If God Is Loving and All-Powerful, Why Does He Allow People to Suffer?
- Considering the Biblical Worldview
- Is the Bible Infallible?
- The Bible's Uniqueness
- The Historicity of Jesus's Resurrection
- Resurrection vs. Resuscitation
- Understanding the Concept of the Trinity
- The Preincarnate Christ Confirms the Three-in-One Nature

- The Ultimate Truth War
- Relative Truth and Tolerance
- The Unique God-Man
- Six Blind Men and the Elephant
- Only One Road Reaches Heaven?
- Amazing Fulfilled Bible Prophecy
- God's Purpose for Prophecy

A Ministry in Christian Apologetics

A few years after I gave my life to Christ, God gave me a passion for lost souls and a desire to study theology. I enrolled in graduate school and majored in Christian apologetics, a branch of theology that defends the truth of Christianity in order to promote the gospel. We studied the extensive evidence for the Christian faith, which is grounded in objective and historical fact—and which far outweighs that of any other religion. For example, Jesus' miraculous resurrection from the dead is the greatest feat in human history. And yet few people take the time to consider the validity of this claim.

One of my professors was the late Dr. A. E. Wilder-Smith. Although he held three doctorates in science, he had a kind approachability. When asked what he considered to be the greatest apologetic for the Christian faith, he replied, "It's showing the love of Christ as you present scriptural truth and evidence for the faith." (That's how I pray that God will use me…and you too!)

After I completed apologetics training and Bible college, God graciously gave me a ministry. True-Way Tracts offers gospel tracts as well as apologetics briefs—evidence-based pamphlets that answer questions posed by truth-seekers (1 Peter 3:15). They are available online at TrueWayTracts.com, and some are cited in this book (see Appendix B for a sample). Our ministry motto is this: "At TWT, we promote the gospel and defend the Christian faith—not only because perishing people need to hear spiritual truth, but also because God is *awesom-azing!*"

OUR SPIRITUAL THIRST

Are you thirsty to have a deeper, more intimate relationship with the living God? Do you want your walk with Him to be more joyful and meaningful? If so, consider reading one or two devotionals in this book each day and meditating on the attributes of God and the Scriptures that illustrate them. Then talk to the Lord about what you read. If you draw near to Him, He will draw near to you (James 4:8) and speak to your heart.

Do you desire for others to know God's love and transforming truth? By spending time with our Lord in frequent prayer, you will naturally reflect His love and pass along His truth. You could also ask Him to bring truth-seekers along your path and empower you to witness of Christ. And if they raise questions about the truth of Christianity, you could share some of the apologetics presented in these pages.

Dear brother or sister in Christ, as you proceed through these chapters, it is my heartfelt desire that you develop a lifelong quest to know our *awesom-azing God*[4] more closely, to showcase His wondrous ways to others, and to become more enamored with Jesus Christ—in whom dwells all the fullness of the Godhead in bodily form (Col. 2:9).

In Jesus's love,

Marilyn Joy Tyner

www.TrueWayTracts.com

www.AwesomazingGod.com

THE FOUNTAIN OF LIVING WATER

QUENCHES OUR SPIRITUAL THIRST

(Jesus Christ declared:)
Whoever drinks of the water that I shall give him
will never thirst. [It] will become in him a fountain
of water springing up into everlasting life.
(John 4:14)

MESMERIZED AT THE WATERFALL

THE THOUGHT OF spending the night with my backpack on the winding asphalt trail so far from home spurred me on. So did my husband's cautionary call.

"Hurry up, let's go!" Tom insisted. "I'm telling you, if you delay even one more minute, we're going to miss our flight home."

I ached for just one more hour to take in the natural beauty of Hawaii's paradise point. Continuous splashings from a towering waterfall mesmerized me—and nearly drowned out Tom's words. My hands gripped the rope guardrail. My resisting feet clung to the blacktop.

As I gasped and blinked at the sights before me, a cool, magnificent mist caressed my face. Random orange blossoms peeked through mossy rocks. Luscious fern fronds displayed a full spectrum of vibrant greens. It was as if a scenery postcard had come to life in multiple dimensions.

For a moment I entertained the temptation to dive into the rippling pool and swim over to the splattering streams of cascading water.

There's no place else I'd rather be, I thought.

This hidden alcove was the last point on our self-guided vacation tour of the tropical Hawaiian rain forest. But Tom and I hadn't allotted nearly enough time for the big island's best attraction, and there was no way we could extend our one-week stay in our neighbor's condo.

There was no solution to my frustration. I felt like an avid hiker, who'd trekked countless miles in the desert heat, following faint trickling sounds coming from the rock formations ahead. And just as she discovered this breathtaking waterfall, darkening skies chased away the sunlight, causing her to race back to camp for safety.

That Hawaiian waterfall was more than simply a gorgeous sight. It touched me spiritually as well, reminding me of one of God's attributes. He is *The Fountain of Living Water*, our Creator. According to the Bible, "He *is* life, while all other things *have* life as a gift from Him."[5]

If we drink of the miraculous "living water" that Jesus freely offers to everyone (see John 4:14), we will live forever with Him. This free gift—of life with endless duration and abundant dimensions[6]—is ours through God's amazing grace.

The symbol of living water also refers to Scripture, which transforms us and quenches our thirsty souls. God's Word is a spiritual gift of endless proportions. We are welcome to dive into it freely anytime, anyplace. There is no time limitation imposed. And we will never reach a point of saturation in the pursuit of God's truth and its application to our lives.

As a redeemed child of God, do you prioritize your day so you can encounter *The Fountain of Living Water* from whom all blessings flow? Do you respond to His invitation to break away from your routine and meet with Him? You can do so by anchoring yourself on a rock near the fountain. Immerse yourself in His Word, delight in Him devotionally, and bathe in His love. Then after you get refreshed, refilled to overflowing, and captivated by His presence, you might even hear yourself telling others, "There's no place else I'd rather be!"

(King David the psalmist wrote:)
[Lord,] in Your presence is fullness of joy;
at Your right hand are pleasures forevermore.
(Ps. 16:11)

DIVINE APPOINTMENT WITH THE MESSIAH

Two thousand years ago, on a scorching-hot day in the desert of Samaria, a wounded woman encountered Jesus one-on-one (see John 4:1–42). Although she was treated by others as a social outcast due to her immoral behavior, Jesus loved her—as He loves all sinners, despite their sins.[7] He could see deep within her an emptiness and a thirst for God.

When the Samaritan woman arrived at Jacob's well to draw water with her pitcher, she saw Jesus sitting there, weary from His travels. He surprised her by asking for a drink. Then He masterfully guided their conversation from physical water to spiritual water, inviting her to drink from the fountain of life.

Physical water represents human pursuits to satisfy our longings (e.g., money, power, careers, or possessions). But Jesus declared, "Whoever drinks of this water will thirst again" (v. 13). On the other hand, living water represents the Holy Spirit and new life. Jesus said the Spirit satisfies and becomes "a fountain of water springing up into everlasting life" (v. 14).

At the defining moment of their conversation, the woman said, "I know that Messiah is coming [and] when He comes, He will tell us all things." Then Jesus revealed to her His identity, saying, "I who speak to you am He" (vv. 25–26).

The long-awaited Messiah stood right before her, igniting her heart like no other could. The spiritual veil lifted from her eyes, and she believed.

If I were in her shoes, I think I would have collapsed in a faint! I can imagine her, with a trembling tone, saying something like this:

> You are the Messiah, and you do know all things! Yes, You're the one foretold by the prophets. You knew all about me, yet you didn't condemn me. No wonder you offered me living water.
>
> Lord, You really do love me. I can see it in Your eyes—and it's a true love. But why would you bother to speak to me, a wretched woman who's been looking for love in all the wrong places?
>
> I can't believe I'm having a conversation with our Deliverer! You actually came in my generation. And to my country. And to Jacob's well. I want You to know that I believe in You and I want to follow You. Please forgive me of my sins.
>
> I'm sure You have much better things to do than talk to me. But please don't go yet. I want to hurry into the village and tell others about You so they can drink Your living water too. They need to know there's hope beyond misery. And they can personally meet the Messiah!

Spiritually alive, the Samaritan woman hastened to the village to share the good news with a new liberation and passion—leaving her water pitcher behind, for she was filled to the brim with living water. As a result, many villagers came to the Wellspring.

Does this nameless woman inspire you? As a believer, you can approach *The Fountain of Living Water* continually. You can marvel at who Jesus is, personally encounter Him, and get refilled with the Holy Spirit (Eph. 5:18). Then you'll be ready to tell thirsty souls that Jesus fully understands them…fully loves them…and will fully quench their thirst.

> (Jesus answered the woman:)
> If you knew the gift of God, and who it is who
> says to you, "Give Me a drink," you would have
> asked Him, and He would have given you living water.
> (John 4:10)

A splash of living water

AN INVITATION TO PLUNGE DEEPER

The living water of God's Word is priceless, pure, refreshing, sparkling, healing, transforming, crystal clear, delicious, cool, thirst quenching, abundant, miraculous, satisfying, and everlasting.

As a beloved believer, you have an open invitation to enjoy this water by diving ever deeper into God's divine revelations. And by drinking of the water consistently, you will enrich your relationship with the living God. This is true whether you are:

- a new believer who recently dipped your feet in the supernatural splashes,

- a young believer who has waded up to your knees in the fresh-flowing streams,

- a mature believer who bathes daily in the living waters near the Fountainhead,

> - a returning believer who is ready to dive back into the waters and get drenched, or
>
> - a missionary-minded believer who enjoys splashing the transforming water onto thirsty souls.
>
> The phrase "living water" carries many rich dimensions of meaning—including Scripture, eternal life, and the Holy Spirit.[8] Since physical water is essential to life, it is no wonder that throughout the pages of the Bible, water symbolizes that which is needed for spiritual life and health.[9]
>
> * * *
>
> *O God, You are my God; early will I seek You;*
> *my soul thirsts for You [for lasting satisfaction];*
> *my flesh longs for You in a dry and*
> *thirsty land where there is no water.*
> *(Ps. 63:1)*

THE ONLY FOUNTAIN OF LIVING WATER

In the book of Jeremiah, God identified Himself as *The Fountain of Living Water*, who alone brings spiritual life and refreshment to people (2:13). Through His prophets, He declared over and over again that He alone is God and there is none like Him (e.g., Isaiah 46:9).

Nevertheless, the Israelites repeatedly turned their backs on the living God and chose to worship powerless pagan gods. In their prosperity, they forgot that Jehovah had delivered them from four hundred years of slavery in Egypt. Although their actions grieved God's heart, rather than giving up on His rebellious people, He continued beckoning them to return. He desired for them to have a loyal relationship with Him as their heavenly Father.

Around 600 BC, God pleaded with the Israelites, "Has any nation ever exchanged its gods for another god, even though its gods are nothing? Yet My people have exchanged their glorious God for worthless idols! The heavens are shocked at such a thing and shrink back in horror and dismay" (Jer. 2:11–12 NLT).

Jehovah went on to identify the two evils His people had committed. First they had given up on Him, the genuine *Fountain of Living Water*. Then they turned to counterfeit sources of water. Out of rocks, they carved cisterns that cracked and couldn't hold water (v. 13).

The same problem exists today in our spiritually mixed-up world. We only have to turn on the television or open a newspaper to find a potpourri of man-based religions and religious philosophies. Some people even invent their own gods—kind of like creating their own Build-a-Bear God.[10] But none of them can quench our spiritual thirst or sustain us or save us.

Our awesom-azing God, whose character never changes, deserves to be worshipped exclusively. As the psalmist wrote, He alone "is to be feared [revered] above all gods. For all the gods of the peoples are idols, but the Lord made the heavens" (Ps. 96:4–5).

It is unpopular today to say there's only one God. And the world's attractions can easily draw our attention away from spending time with the Lord, and keeping Him first in our lives. But if we listen for and heed His beckoning call, our returned joy and reignited light will attract others to Him.

Why not ask God to use you and others to help awaken our culture so that more people can hear His heartbeat of love and His words of eternal life? He loves to answer such kingdom-advancing prayers! Then precious souls for whom Christ died will no longer need to drink stale water in cracked basins. They can drink pure living water from the ever-flowing Fountain.

You are awesome. You're amazing. You're the awesom-azing God. You're the fount of living water, and nothing else satisfies.

> [My people] have forsaken Me, the fountain
> of living waters, and hewn themselves cisterns
> —broken [basins] that can hold no water.
> (Jer. 2:13)

THIRSTY TO THE BONE

Have you ever experienced extreme physical thirst? Were you thirsty to the bone, so to speak? Ready to guzzle a quart of ice water if you could only locate one? Anne Graham Lotz no doubt experienced that degree of thirstiness on the first day of her marriage while enduring face-dripping heat on a road trip. The full account appears in her book *Just Give Me Jesus*.[11] Here is a summary of her funny-after-the-fact story.

> On the first day of Anne's marriage to Danny Lotz, they drove along an interstate highway to Atlanta in 95-degree weather. Noticing that the fuel needle was hovering close to E, she said in her sweetest, most submissive voice, "Danny darling, the gas is getting low. Don't you think we should stop and fill up?"
>
> "No, no," he replied emphatically. "We have plenty of gas."
>
> A few miles later, when the needle dropped farther, she suggested, "Danny darling, the gas gauge is registering below empty. Why don't we stop and fill up?"
>
> "This car always has more gas than the gauge indicates," he responded.
>
> Soon after, the car lurched, popped, and coughed, then glided to a stop. They had run out of gas!
>
> Wanting to be protective of his new bride, charming Danny rolled up all the windows and locked the doors to

keep her safe inside. Then he jogged down the road out of sight. Forty-five scorching, smelly minutes later, he reappeared in a tow truck with a can of gasoline. While Danny poured gas into their tank, the truck driver peered at Anne's dripping face through the closed windows.

As Anne gasped for air, Danny opened the door with a big smile and jumped in. He confidently turned the key in the ignition. Nothing happened. Though he tried repeatedly, he couldn't make the motor turn over. The battery had died, and the tow truck was gone.

Anne's new husband rolled up the windows, locked the doors, and once again jogged into the distance. The heat outside the car was nothing compared to the heat inside Anne. She felt frustrated, miserable, and nauseated, and wondered what she had gotten herself into!

Another forty-five minutes later, hope appeared on the horizon. The tow truck returned, and the mechanic helped Danny jump-start the battery. This time, however, the attendant didn't leave until the car was safely running.

(Wow, what an introduction to married life! I hope Danny scored a few points with his new bride by at least bringing her an ice-cold drink after leaving her in that sweltering heat so long.)

In addition to the physical thirst that all people experience, we all have a spiritual thirst for God. He created us with a God-shaped void in our hearts that nothing else can fill. If we seek after Him, we can share an ever-deepening love with Him and find fulfillment in Him.[12]

Take a few minutes today to reflect on the wonderful truth that you personally know Jesus Christ—the missing piece—who fills the emptiness in your spirit. Why not thank Him for inviting you to drink from the waters that spring up into everlasting life (John 4:14)? Because you heard His call and responded to

Him, you are now privileged beyond measure. He quenches your thirsty soul. And your relationship with the Lord of all creation will never end.

> I am the Alpha and the Omega, the Beginning
> and the End. I will give of the fountain of
> the water of life freely to him who thirsts
> [who recognizes his spiritual longing].
> (Rev. 21:6)

A splash of apologetics to share

RELIGION VS. RELATIONSHIP

Religion is man reaching up to God, trying to become acceptable to Him by doing some form of good works.

Christianity is merciful God reaching down to man, sending His Son to unite us with Him by His grace.

* * *

In effect, Jesus Christ says: "I did not come to offer a religion. I did not come to offer a system of rules by which a person reaches the right destination. I am not so much interested in pointing you to a place as I am pointing you to a Person and a relationship. That is the key…Anyone can come into My presence because I am the way. I have come so that you can have the indwelling presence of my Holy Spirit."[13]

—Ravi Zacharias

Sitting in Shock in the Emergency Room

Will my beloved stepdaughter ever wake up? Will she ever walk again? As I sat in the ICU waiting room, I couldn't believe that my "treasured daughter" (a title I affectionately call her) had been shot in the stomach by a teenage gang-girl on drugs.

Fifteen or so family members sat with my husband and me, intensely awaiting updates. Her surgeon had told us that she flat-lined for four or five minutes soon after checking herself into Emergency and then collapsing.

I sank onto a lobby couch and opened my Bible to the book of Acts. Since it is filled with miraculous works of the Holy Spirit, I decided to read every page to find a specific passage to pray for Sherry.

Two verses jumped off the page. Peter and John were taken into custody and questioned by the Sanhedrin (Jewish court) about a crippled beggar who was miraculously healed through Peter's prayer. "By what power or by what name have you done this?" they asked (Acts 4:7).

Filled with the Holy Spirit, Peter replied that the lame man stood whole "by the name of Jesus Christ of Nazareth," whom they crucified but whom God had raised from the dead (v. 10).

Without a moment's hesitation, I asked God to touch Sher so she could "stand whole again by the powerful name of Jesus Christ of Nazareth." I didn't pray to a nebulous god, or a distant god, or a god of a religious system. I prayed to the supreme God, *The Fountain of Living Water* who gives life.

I wasn't the only person praying for Sher's recovery. But at the moment I prayed that Scripture, God gave me an extra measure of faith that He would heal her wounds. And He stepped in! Sher's condition teetered for a few days, but after three weeks in the hospital she was released. She even walked to the car without assistance. Praise God, she could *stand whole again!*

Are you ready to call on our awesom-azing God in times of crisis? He is ready to hear from you. And He will already be on the scene when you call. After all, He is mighty in power and assures us that He will grant any petition that lines up with His will (1 John 5:14–15). And if we focus more on His ability than our problems, surely our faith will increase an extra measure.

[God] is able to do exceedingly abundantly
above all that we ask or think, according
to the power that works in us.
(Eph. 3:20)

JESUS, THE SPIRITUAL ROCK

The Feast of Tabernacles commemorates how God satisfied the Israelites' tremendous thirst during their forty years of wilderness wanderings. A rock followed them, providing life-giving water (Ex. 17:5–6). When Moses struck the rock with his rod, water gushed out and ran in the dry areas like a river (Ps. 105:41).

God later revealed that the rock in the wilderness represented the presence of the preincarnate Christ (1 Cor. 10:4). Just think. The only person who ever *lived before He was born* was divinely satisfying the thirst of God's people.

Now fast forward to a spectacular event in the first century AD, 1,500 years later. Jesus preached from the temple in Jerusalem where thousands of Jews were gathered to celebrate the Feast of Tabernacles (John 7:37–39). When the priests poured out water on the pavement as part of the ceremony, Jesus stood and cried out before the worshippers that if anyone would believe in Him, He would give them living water—the Holy Spirit (v. 39).

The Savior of the world was giving a firsthand gospel call![14] The Water of Life—that spiritual rock in the desert—publicly declared Himself to be the promised Messiah. He offered to satisfy the inner thirst of anyone who would come to Him.

In his book *Living Water*, Chuck Smith describes the human thirst for God, which Jesus proclaimed that day:

> Deep down in the spirit of every [person] resides an unquenchable need for God…Jesus is the answer to our thirst. He is the only One who can satisfy our thirst for God [and] bring fulfillment and completion. He is in essence saying, "In the deepest part of your being you need God. Come to Me!"[15]

In the wilderness, God told Moses not to strike the rock a second time, but merely speak to the rock and it would yield water (Num. 20:8). His instruction carried deep symbolism. Someday Jesus would be crucified on the cross for our sins, and He would never need to be struck again. His work would be finished once and for all. Nothing could be added to it.

The Fountain of Living Water provides us with truth, wisdom, comfort, guidance, counsel, and refillings with His Holy Spirit. Our Bibles are bottomless reservoirs of living water, and Jesus will speak to us through the Scriptures if we seek and listen. Why not make it a frequent practice to speak to the Rock? If you do, Jesus will continue to shower you with His goodness and fill you to overflowing with His Spirit.

(Jesus cried out:)
If anyone thirsts, let Him come to Me and drink.
He who believes in Me…out of his heart [his
innermost being] will flow rivers of living water.
(John 7:37–38)

ON THE EDGE OF MAGIC

Despite fiery-trial circumstances, my friend Rupert trusted that God would see him through his season of homelessness. Rupert (a nickname he chose) had served in the Air Force with my son, and over time began to call me his spiritual mom. Although our family lost contact with him for several years after he moved to Las Vegas, he reappeared through an e-mail. A few months after we reconnected, Rupert spent every dime he had on a used laptop from a pawn shop and a one-way bus ticket to San Diego.

He went straight to St. Vincent de Paul's, a transitional facility he had located online, which offers a sixty-day program to help people overcome homelessness. Upon arrival, he was told to come back in ten days to receive a bed assignment.

Rupert was forced to live on the sidewalk and fare the elements. His priority became getting out of the March cold and rain, so he found temporary shelter under a bridge where homeless men and women camped in bed rolls. His longer-range priority was finding a way to get on "Viability Road" (as he called it), to get back on his feet financially.

One day, he sent me a comical e-mail that assured me he was still optimistic about God and his life. Here's an excerpt from it:

> Whenever I see any kind of cheese, typically I make a U-turn. So you aren't gonna believe this incident at the shelter, or maybe you will. I went over to St. Vincent's for lunch. As I waited in line, pretty hungry, I overheard the meal was Chili-Mac. Uh-oh! I hoped it was the variety without cheese. I was wrong. I saw people enjoying their food, with goo hanging off their forks. The goo was cheese. Eeeewww.
>
> As I got to the front, the serving pan they scooped the food out of had cheese on top. There were puddles of cheese in the middle and cheese just everywhere I looked. So I figured for me it would be only bread, veggies, and juice for lunch. I grabbed my tray and sat down.
>
> I looked at my Chili-Mac. It didn't look cheesy. I didn't even smell any cheese. Then I tasted it with a minuscule bite off the edge of my fork. It had no cheese! If it did, it was so diluted, I tasted nothing but chili flavor and beef. I took a fork full. They scooped this out of the same pan that almost turned my stomach. But there was *no cheese* whatever!

I had only mentioned in my head that I guessed it was gonna be veggies and juice for me. I don't think I even whined to God about the cheese, but He must have heard me. The tray before mine was all goo-ed up, and the tray after mine was goo-ed up, but mine had no cheese at all. It blew me away!

I've been singing the old Monkees' song "I'm a Believer" with new lyrics: *Then I saw His hand. Now I'm a believer. I can't understand. I try in my mind. I'm in love (ooh, aah). I'm a believer, I wouldn't leave Him if I could.*

Marilyn, you were the one to look at the small miracles He does in our lives, and I'll be a son of a gun, I'm sold. Just thought I'd share, because today was on the edge of magic.

After I chuckled out loud for a while, Rupert's predicament tugged at my heart strings. My capable friend was homeless and penniless. I trusted that success was around the corner for him because he was reading a daily devotional filled with living water.

Perhaps you are struggling with life's difficulties today. If so, be encouraged that God carries us through seasons of hardship and provides for our needs (Phil. 4:19). And He uses the valleys in our lives to stretch our faith—which is valued by Him and brings us eternal benefits. In the meantime, stay in fellowship with God, keep drinking the water of His Word, and stand on His glorious promise that He works all things out for the good of every believer. After all, God is awesom-azing, so *we wouldn't leave Him if we could!*

We know that all things work together for good
to those who love God, to those who are
the called according to His purpose.
(Rom. 8:28)

A splash of apologetics to share

WHICH RELIGION IS THE OLDEST?

Christianity predates all religions, since: (a) The Bible refers to the beginning of all creation, including the first two human beings; (b) Jesus testified to the accuracy of Genesis and the existence of Adam and Eve (Matt. 19:4–6); (c) The Holy Spirit inspired Moses to write Genesis c. 1500 BC, by compiling earlier records passed down; (d) Before the foundation of the world, God decided to create people in His own image and to mercifully redeem them after they fell (Gen. 1:26; Rev. 13:8).[16]

—Don Stewart, apologist

(For an overview of what sets Christianity apart from "religion," see Appendix B and the endnote.[17])

LIVING WATER OF ETERNAL LIFE

Rupert e-mailed me soon after the Chili-Mac incident. Late one windy night, he sat in the dark on a bridge in San Diego, looking over the edge and crying. He tried to stay warm wrapped inside his hoodie, but still shivered in the cold. I'm not sure whether it was a bridge over water or traffic. But the tone of his e-mail seemed to indicate he considered jumping.

A Honda Accord pulled up beside him, and a little Hispanic girl jumped out and offered him a free sweater. Rupert gladly accepted it. She smiled and asked if he wanted prayer, to which he replied, "Yes, please." (I wish I could have heard her prayer!) After telling him the name of her church, she hopped back into the car. I suspect the sweater warmed his heart even more than his shoulders.

I wondered if that little girl was an angel sent from above to help Rupert, perhaps in answer to one of my prayers for him or to someone else's prayers (see Heb. 1:14).

When Rupert's ten-day waiting period was over, he returned to St. Vincent's shelter, eager to be assigned a bed and get cleaned up. He had endured ten horrific days living on the sidewalks. When he arrived, however, he was told that the ten-day wait was merely to get his name on the four-week waiting list. Too many homeless people were trying to get in at the same time.

According to Rupert's e-mail, he was heading to the pawn shop to sell his laptop—his only contact with the outside world. Realizing that I might never hear from him again, I prayed fervently that he would not jump off some bridge and that he would connect with me again.

At least I had some big-picture consolation. Several years ago, Rupert had heeded God's call to come to Him and drink of the living water of eternal life (Isa. 55:1–3). He received Jesus Christ, who bridged the gap for him—between holy God and less-than-perfect people (2 Cor. 5:18). So even if he did jump, my friend would land in the palm of God's hand, never to be separated from His love.

I prayed, *Thank You, awesom-azing God, for Rupert's salvation and for ministering to him. You know every detail of his life, even what kind of thread was woven into the sweater from the little girl. Please weave the broken threads of his life back together, according to Your plan.*

Have you recently worshipped the God of our salvation? Have you praised our merciful Lord lately for giving you, or someone else, eternal life? After all, He bought us at an unthinkable price (1 Cor. 6:20). And He called us out of this spiritually confused and pluralistic world to worship Him—the genuine *Fountain of Living Water.*

Ho! Everyone who thirsts, come to the waters…
Incline your ear, and come to Me.
Hear, and your soul shall live.
(Isa. 55:1–3)

A WATER BOY CARRYING BUCKETS

Michael is a wonderful guy who has nearly completed a seven-year sentence of incarceration. Basically, drugs took him down and stripped him of most everything he owned and loved.

I'd met Michael before he went to jail, and he asked me to come visit him there. When I discovered he was receptive to hearing about the Lord, I delivered him a cool cup of living water every couple of weeks by offering encouragement from God's Word. I also mailed Michael some gospel tracts, and he began faithfully reading a Bible.

A few months after my first visit, a fellow inmate told Michael that God loved him and then invited him to receive Christ. And he did! Michael came to Jesus and freely drank the water of life (Rev. 22:17).

After my friend got transferred from the county jail to a state prison, he shared living water of Scripture with his cellmate Jerold, who also drank of it and quenched his spiritual thirst. A couple of years later, Michael transferred to another facility, where he shared living water with Bobby, who also received the life-giving water. Bobby then started studying the Bible, and in time he became the leader of a Bible study with forty men. Thirsty souls began drinking in the Word of God, finding fulfillment and freedom in Christ.

According to my last letter from Michael, he has transferred to yet another facility. And He is carrying a bucket of living water with him. Needless to say, there is a rippling effect going on!

We read in Matthew 25 that the Son of Man will return to earth in His glory with all the holy angels to judge the nations (vv. 31–46). Our King will sit on the throne and separate people like sheep from goats. (The sheep will inherit the kingdom because they personally accepted the sacrifice of Jesus.) Those saved sheep who then went on to minister to God's people in need of food, drink, clothing, a place to stay, or a visit in prison, displayed servants' hearts in tune with God's heart—and thereby ministered to the King as well (v. 40).

That passage has personal application to us today. If we spend time with our King in prayer, so that our hearts line up with His servant's heart, and if we then go on to serve needy people, we will be serving the Lord at the same time.

Are you willing to follow God's leading in serving others in Christ's name and with His love? Even if you don't have huge financial resources, you can always pass along kindness or carry a bucket of living water to thirsty souls. You need only ask the Holy Spirit to open doors for you to share a Scripture, or a personal testimony, or perhaps offer to pray for someone. When you do, those in need will become much better off, and the ultimate Servant will someday look into your face—as He will with Michael—and reward you with a royal smile.

> I was hungry and you gave Me food;
> I was thirsty and you gave Me drink…
> I say to you, inasmuch as you did it to one of the
> least of these My brethren, you did it to Me.
> (Matt. 25:35–40)

TOO MUCH HEAVEN?

A dermatologist I know, Dr. Dao, sponsors orphans in Vietnam. On one of her trips to the orphanage, she packed several canisters of Almond Roca to give the children to bless them with a special treat. They seemed thrilled. But one little boy would only accept a single piece of the candy. When Dr. Dao asked why he refused to take more, he humbly replied, "It's too much heaven!" He wanted to savor that one sweet treat, fully appreciating it.

After I heard this precious story, the Vietnamese boy's remark and his heart of gratitude lingered in my thoughts. What if a conveyer belt transported full canisters of Almond Roca from a factory straight to me, quickly and nonstop? There's no way I could enjoy that much candy all at once!

Similarly, when drinking the living water of God's Word, it is helpful to pace ourselves in order to appreciate its richness. Our goal is not the quantity we consume each day, for we need time to process its wonders. Perhaps a few drops (verses) or a few cups (chapters) at a time are plenty. Then we can meditate on them and ask the Holy Spirit to show us how they apply to our lives.

Understanding the Bible, and how to live by it, is a lifetime endeavor. We will never be able to plumb the depths of its meaning, since God's wisdom and ways are unsearchable (Rom. 11:33). Perhaps that's partly why Scripture tells us it will take all of eternity for God to show us the exceeding riches of His grace toward us in Christ Jesus (Eph. 2:7).

We can, however, enjoy feasting on God's fresh manna each day, knowing that more will be supplied on the following day, and the next day, and the next. And if we hide God's words in our hearts, we will know Him more…please Him more…and live for His glory more.

The Fountain of Living Water supplies His children with spiritual blessings that are far too wonderful to comprehend. Even when we read about them in Scripture, it can be "too much heaven" for us to process. Yet we can accept one small piece of divine grace each day from our loving Creator—and thank Him with a grateful heart.

Thank You, Lord, for splashing upon us Your tender mercies, which are new and fresh every morning. Great is Your faithfulness. You deserve our deepest devotion.

> Through the Lord's mercies we are not
> consumed, because His compassions fail not.
> They are new every morning; great is Your faithfulness.
> (Lam. 3:22–23)

PRAYING TO OUR AWESOM-AZING GOD

This chapter showcased glorious facets of God's character: He is life, and the source of all life, and He is holy.

Are you ready to praise Him right now for your mega-blessings of life and rebirth? If so, below is a suggested prayer. And if you're ready to take a deeper plunge in your relationship with Christ, you could ask Him to fill you to overflowing with His Holy Spirit[18] (see the second paragraph below). If you do, surely your walk with Him will become more fervent, your service to Him more fruitful, and your treasures in heaven more plentiful.

Lord God, You are holy and worthy of all glory and honor and praise. I worship You as The Fountain of Living Water, who gave me life physically and spiritually. Thank You for making me a new creation, cleansed by the precious blood of Jesus. Now I know the true and living God! And I worship You in spirit and in truth. Thank You also for quenching my thirst by guiding me into more spiritual truth each time I immerse myself in the water of Your Word.

Lord, will You fill me to overflowing with Your Holy Spirit right now? I want to walk in deeper devotion to You with more of Jesus in my heart. Lead me in Your service, and help me pass on Your living water to other thirsty souls. I know that even one drop, when offered to someone in the powerful name of Jesus Christ, can lead to life everlasting. Thank You for Your wellspring of infinite love containing blessings that never end. In Jesus' name, amen.

OUR MATCHLESS KING

Treats Us as His Royal Sons and Daughters

BEJEWELED WITH BIG BLESSINGS

"It's nice to meet you, Hannah," I said to the lovely middle-aged woman sitting next to me, after I glanced at her name tag. "How long have you been a Christian?" Little did I know, God was about to "bejewel" both of us with blessings. Our small-group discussion had ended in the Bible study, and hundreds of women shuffled into the sanctuary for a time of corporate worship.

"Oh, I'm not a Christian yet," replied Hannah with an endearing smile. "But I really *want* to be. Yesterday I asked the man working in the bookstore how I could become one. He told me to come to this women's Bible study and they'd tell me."

"Well, I'm so glad you're here," I said with joy filling my heart and spilling over. "I'd love to share and pray with you—maybe right after the message by the pastor's wife." I knew the Lord had matched us up, for I had an eighteen-month-long burden to introduce someone to the King of all kings.

My friend Jeannette walked over and joined our conversation, and the three of us sat together for the Bible lecture. Afterward, our trio took a seat in the last row of the empty church and entered the throne room of grace. Bowing before our heavenly King, I could almost hear angels' praises erupt in celebration as Hannah received Jesus into her heart. And through that profound uniting, "astounding spiritual riches"became hers[19] (see Eph. 1:3).

Just two weeks earlier, I had poured out my heart to the Lord on the back porch of my home in the Midwest, while a moving van loaded up our belongings to transport them back home to California. My husband's job had unexpectedly ended, and I was grieving over more than just that loss.

"Lord, I thought You placed the desire on my heart to lead someone to You here in Indiana. And now it's too late. Maybe I missed out on the opportunity because I didn't hear Your call. I'm so sorry." Although I had enjoyed sowing seeds of God's truth (Matt. 13) during my stint in Indiana, I longed to personally introduce someone to the Royal Ruler of heaven and earth. Yet as *Our Matchless King* already knew, He was about to fulfill my longing, as well as Hannah's desire to start a relationship with Him.

When God sets up divine appointments, He providentially works at both ends. He is looking for people who will worship Him in spirit and in truth (John 4:23–24). And at just the right time, He will connect a diligent seeker with a willing proclaimer. The Roman centurion Cornelius, for example, had been praying to the God of Israel with a seeking heart. And the Holy Spirit led Peter to Caesarea to preach to Cornelius and his household. As a result, they all received Jesus as their Savior and were marvelously saved (Acts 10:1–11:18).

Even though not all believers have experienced the joy of praying with someone to receive Jesus, He assures us that someday the sowers and the reapers will rejoice together in heaven when we see the fruit of our labors (John 4:35–38).

As a bejeweled son or daughter of the King—ornamented with His blessings and arrayed with His presence—do you share God's Word? If so, then you know the joy of partnering with Jesus as He builds His church. If you've never prayed with someone to receive Christ (see Rom. 10:9–10), why not enter God's throne room and ask Him to lead a "searcher" across your path and inspire your conversation. If that person someday joins the royal family, he or she will be praising *Our Matchless King*—adorned with mega-blessings.

> Sing praises to our King, sing praises!
> For God is the King of all the earth; sing
> praises with understanding. God reigns over
> the nations; God sits on His holy throne.
> (Ps. 47:6–8)

FROM THE CRADLE, TO THE CROSS, TO THE CROWN

The magi from the East, commonly spoken of as "three wise men," followed the Bethlehem star. Somehow they knew it was a sign of the coming King of the Jews. They traveled a long distance from Persia or Babylon, for months or years, not merely to honor an earthly ruler but to worship the promised Jewish Messiah.

What convinced them to make this arduous journey to greet the Christ child? As astrologers, they studied the stars to determine the future. Most likely they also studied Hebrew messianic prophecies, such as those based on Daniel's visions five centuries earlier while he lived in Babylon. Daniel predicted both the time and location of the coming Messiah, whose dominion would be everlasting (see Dan. 7:13–14; 9:24–26).

Evidently these dignitaries had hearts seeking the living God, for He revealed to them a supernatural guiding star. Honoring the Infant King, they brought gifts fit for royalty: gold, frankincense, and myrrh. Their gifts represented Jesus' threefold office. Gold for a king, frankincense for a priest, and myrrh for a martyred prophet.[20]

In the grand scheme, God predetermined all the details surrounding the earthly arrival of Jesus. At just the proper moment, in the fullness of time (Gal. 4:4), God sent forth His Son to redeem mankind. When Christ stepped from heaven into time and space, He passed from the cradle…to the cross…to the crown of glory.[21] As a result, all true believers are part of His kingdom.

Aren't you grateful that God loves to meet genuine seekers wherever they are and draw them to His Son?

How privileged we are to live on this side of the cross. Unlike the magi, we don't need to travel afar to seek *Our Matchless King*. We have instant access to Him through prayer and the Scripture. Like those wise men, is it your heart's desire to worship the prophesied King? And pursue the Person who's the very centerpiece of Scripture (Heb. 10:7)? If so, ask Him to give you a greater sense of wonder as you read your Bible. For He longs to reveal Himself, His love, and His kingdom truths to those who follow His lead.

> Where is He who has been born King of the Jews?
> For we have seen His star in the East and have
> [followed it and] come to worship Him.
> (Matt. 2:2)

ICY FEET AT MIDNIGHT

Last summer, I "kicked off" a chain reaction of physical injuries. It began when I rounded the corner of our laundry room too fast and booted a cardboard box with my little toe. Ouch! The doctor advised me to tape my broken blue toe to the adjacent toe and wear a protective bootie for six weeks. That sounded simple enough. However, I tried to facilitate healing by shifting my weight to the inside of my foot (away from my throbbing toe), which inflamed ligaments in the arches.

That painful condition (called fasciitis) lasted for many months. It flared up the tendonitis in my knees, which led to ice packs and resulted in freezer burns. Next came physical therapy, followed by shoe orthotics. *Will the dominoes ever stop falling?* I complained.

Time after time, I got out of bed in the middle of the night to ice the inflammation in my arches, which sent icy shock waves through my feet. One evening I asked the Lord if He would please heal my injuries so I could get some uninterrupted sleep. Then the Holy Spirit reminded me that I had been enjoying special prayer time with the Lord, sitting at His feet during my twenty-minute treatments.

Did I really want to give up that midnight meeting with my beloved Savior, triggered by my screaming ligaments? Was this an opportunity I should be treasuring instead of grumbling about?

Sometimes God presents us with tests that prove our love for Him. Abraham passed a huge test of love, and faith, when he offered up his son Isaac on Mount Moriah (Gen. 22). He believed that God could raise Isaac from the dead in order to fulfill a promise He had made to bring descendants through the line of his promised son (see Heb. 11:17–19).

I decided not to complain about my feet anymore. Prayer is intimate conversations with our awesom-azing God. In the stillness of the night, there are no distractions and His voice is more perceptible than during busy daytime hours.

Eventually, the pain in my feet dissipated. However, I still occasionally get up to pray in the middle of the night. Now that my feet no longer awaken me, my alarm clock is the gentle nudge of the Holy Spirit. And whenever I meet with *Our Matchless King* while the stars are still out, it's always a royal experience.

Does it boggle your mind that the Lord of the universe wants to communicate to you personally? If you listen for His still small voice, you will be more likely to hear from Him when the clatter of the world has calmed down or is on hold. You might receive revelations from the Holy Spirit, showing how certain Scriptures apply to your life issues. And your heart may leap with joy—no matter what time of the day it is.

> Behold, the Lord…was not in the wind; and after
> the wind an earthquake, but the Lord was not in the
> earthquake; and after the earthquake a fire, but the Lord
> was not in the fire; and after the fire a still small voice.
> (1 Kings 19:11–12)

A praise song to our King and Friend

JESUS, THE MATCHLESS KING

My Jesus, You are the Matchless King.
How I long to give to You my everything,
No one compares; help me to share
Your matchless grace,
    So all may come and seek Your holy face.

My Jesus, You are the Matchless King.
Humbly I bow to You; my life I bring.
With a grateful heart and a brand-new start
I'm here to serve,
    To shine Your light and love as You deserve.

My Jesus, You are the Matchless King.
I worship You in spirit, and in truth I sing.
I praise Your name, with love proclaim
Your faithfulness.
        Let all Your people sing, let heaven's voices ring,
        For You're the Lord, and You're the Matchless King.

(Chorus)
The Matchless King, Jesus, the Matchless King, my Friend.
The Matchless King, Jesus, You alone are the Matchless King.[22]

RUNNING INTO THE THRONE ROOM

Kay Arthur, a prominent Bible teacher and author, tells of an overwhelming time in her life when she strove to be supermom—single and trying to work and go to school. In her mind's eye one day, she saw a scene.

A little girl ran for her daddy, with tears streaming down her face and banged-up, bloody knees on her skinny legs. She ran down a huge corridor with marble walls and heavenly light spilling through the windows. At the end of the hallway were massive gold doors protected by guards with great spears. Kay writes:

> I knew that the little girl was me, and that I was running toward the very throne room of El Elyon, sovereign ruler of the universe. Yet I was the daughter of the King of kings, so when the guards saw me coming, they swung open those doors and let me run in. There I was, weeping and running into the very presence of El Elyon. I heard the cherubim and the seraphim crying out, "Holy, holy, holy, Lord God Almighty! Heaven and earth are full of Thy glory!"

> Many bowed before the throne, and court was in ses-
> sion, but I just ran and ran and didn't stop. Because the
> One on the throne was not only Elohim, my Creator, not
> only El Elyon, the sovereign ruler of the universe, but He
> was also my El Shaddai, my all-sufficient One.
>
> I could just see myself running up the wide stairs to
> that glorious throne—two steps at a time—crying "Abba,
> Father! Daddy!"
>
> And I could see Him stopping everything, opening
> His arms wide and just gathering me to His chest, saying,
> "There, there, My precious child. Let Me wipe away those
> tears. Tell your Father all about it."[23]

As a son or daughter of the King of kings, do you run into His throne room in times of need? Whenever you approach Him in prayer, He will welcome you with outstretched arms and give you immediate attention. He will treat you as His royal treasure, viewing you as His own inheritance. And for that instant, it may seem as if the King on high stops everything else to attend to your banged-up, bloody knees.

> [May we realize] the riches of the glory
> of His inheritance in the saints [that God's
> people are His rich and glorious inheritance].
> (Eph. 1:18)

QUEEN ESTHER AND THE KING

Esther, the newly appointed queen of Persia (c. 483 BC), was ter-rified when she learned the news that all Jews (her people) would be annihilated on a designated day by royal orders (Est. 3:12–13). King Xerxes, her husband, had been manipulated into signing that irrevocable decree. What could she do to stop it? Should she reveal her Jewish nationality? Should she request the king's favor and risk losing her life?

According to Persian protocol, the king could order her execution if she appeared before his throne without a summons. The chance of hearing "Off with her head!" was great. Her only hope was if he extended his royal scepter to her, granting permission for her to approach and present her plea.

Esther's uncle Mordecai,[24] who had raised her as his own daughter, stirred her into action with this staggering possibility: "Yet who knows whether you have come to the kingdom for such a time as this?" (4:14). Had God providentially placed her in the royal court in order to deliver the Jews?

After considering the notion, Esther replied, "I will go to the king, which is against the law; and if I perish, I perish!" (4:16). She recognized the gravity of the situation and accepted her high calling.

To prepare for her appeal to King Xerxes, Esther called for a three-day fast by her personal maids and all the Jews in the empire. As a result, she received the king's approval to present her request. Upon revealing to him the villain and his evil plot, he authorized a new decree allowing the Jews to at least defend themselves on the day of the attack (8:8–11).

From our perspective, we can see that God had arranged natural things to correspond with His supernatural will. He raised Esther from obscurity to become the queen of Persia by winning a royal beauty pageant. Then He used her mightily in that position to save her entire nation.

And there's more! Esther's courageous plea to the king preserved the messianic line. For God had promised that the Messiah would come through the Jewish race to redeem mankind. And centuries later, despite relentless spiritual warfare, He indeed came for us.

Our God is faithful to perform all His promises. If we surrender our will to Him, He will accomplish great things in and through us because His providential hand will be upon us.

Lord, I'm amazed that You can even use an ordinary person like me to accomplish extraordinary things. By Your grace, help me to surrender my plans to You each day. And help me make wise choices that will please You and serve to extend Your kingdom. I pray this as Your loving servant. In Jesus' name, amen.

Who knows whether you have come
to the kingdom [whether God has placed
you right where you are] for such a time as this?
(Est. 4:14)

"IF IT PLEASES THE KING"

At the crucial moment when Queen Esther stood before the Persian king to present her plea—no doubt quaking in her satin slippers—she carefully prefaced her petition with these words: "If I have found favor in the sight of the king, and if it pleases the king to grant my petition and fulfill my request…" (Est. 5:8; see also 7:3).

Thankfully, we need not quake in our slippers or shoes or boots when we approach *Our Matchless King* as His beloved sons and daughters. Consider these marvelous truths about His invitation for us to come into His throne room in prayer (Heb. 4:15–16):

- He extends grace and mercy to us whenever we approach Him.

- He grants our every petition that lines up with His will and timing.

- He responds to our requests based on His infinite wisdom and love.

- He welcomes us personally and enjoys our fellowship with Him.

For truth-seekers, the King extends His scepter of saving grace, freely offering them the opportunity to become righteous in Christ (2 Cor. 5:21). They need only to say a simple, heartfelt prayer such as this:

"If it pleases the King, will You grant my petition and fulfill my request? Forgive my sins and cleanse me. I gladly receive Jesus Christ as my Lord and Savior."

As Scripture promises, the King will then reply, *Enter into My kingdom. I've been waiting for you.* The gospel of grace requires nothing on our part, because God's Son has already purchased our salvation (Heb. 9:22–26). As the popular hymn says, "Naught of good that I have done, nothing but the blood of Jesus."[25]

Someday we will be casting crowns of praise, honor, and glory before the Lord's throne. I wonder if we will be joining the twenty-four elders who fall down before our King, casting their crowns in worship (Rev. 4:10). And when we, too, fall down in adoration—whether on our knees or flat on our faces—I wonder if we will be close enough to see the marks of love on His nail-scarred feet.

Dear Lord of heaven, I come before Your throne and praise You for purchasing my salvation. I can barely comprehend the great price You paid to offer me saving grace. Thank You also for Your enabling grace that helps me carry out Your decrees. What an awesom-azing God You are. I exalt You as my King, and I cast crowns of praise at Your feet right now.

Let us therefore come boldly to the throne
of grace, that we may obtain mercy and
find grace to help in time of need.
(Heb. 4:16)

Splashes of living water and apologetics

THE MESSIANIC LINE PRESERVED

When Esther interceded for her people, almighty God intervened. He canceled the satanic attempt to destroy the entire Jewish race.

Centuries later, the King of the Jews stepped onto the scene. Jesus made His triumphal entry into Jerusalem in AD 33, publicly declaring Himself to be the long-awaited Messiah. He arrived on the exact date that the prophet Daniel had predicted 483 years earlier. (See Dan. 9:24–26 and Luke 19:28–40.)

On that historic day (referred to now as Palm Sunday), the King humbly rode into the city on the colt of a donkey, just as the prophet Zechariah had predicted so long ago. And the people cried out "Hosanna in the highest!" (See Ps. 118:25–26; Zech. 9:9; and Matt. 21:4–9.)

Consider this: if all the Jews had been annihilated in Queen Esther's day, as planned, our Savior would not have been born. Yet God's Word is trustworthy, His prophets were accurate, and absolutely nothing can thwart the plan of almighty God.

(For the date calculations of Daniel's startling three-part prophecy, see the endnote.[26])

PETITIONING THE SOVEREIGN KING

I continued to bring my work-displaced friend, Rupert, before the throne room in prayer. After two weeks with no correspondence, he sent me an e-mail update. He hadn't sold his laptop after all, but he had experienced an Internet access problem. Thankfully, Rupert was back on track with a strengthened heart.

As it turned out, God had ministered to him once again. While last time He sent a little girl *above* the bridge, this time He sent a retired Baptist preacher *under* the bridge. "Ole Sandy" opened up his Bible and splashed on Rupert the living water of God's wisdom and encouragement.

Although he was still living on the sidewalk, Rupert remarked with his typical wittiness, "God actually takes time from running the universe to keep me safe." He also told me he was "back in the boat with God" and that his faith was still strong.

My husband and I invited him to be a guest in our home for a couple of days, and he accepted. I drove to San Diego to pick him up at the homeless resource center. In my SUV, I forged my way through streets filled with busy traffic, homeless people, and confusion. Prayer and tenacity helped me locate Rupert near Father Joe's chapel. Smiling big, he hopped into my passenger seat.

While driving up the freeway together, we petitioned the heavenly King for guidance and made our plans: eat lunch, shop for clothing at thrift stores, check out job possibilities, wash his clothes, then attend an evening Bible study—all of which we accomplished. Whew!

We searched in three thrift shops for a pair of shoes he could wear with jeans and his one pair of interview slacks. But men's shoes were sparse on the shelves, and the few available were miniature or giant in size. At our last stop, one shoe fit like a glove. A high quality loafer, priced at only $5.00, met all our criteria. But its mate was missing.

After we exhausted our search, the counter clerk, who had overheard our conversation, shouted to us that she found a men's shoe at the cash register. *Could it possibly be?* I wondered. Sure enough, it turned out to be the estranged mate. Together we thanked God, who had shown us His care.

That night I prayed, *Thank You, Jesus, for answering our prayer for a suitable pair of shoes for Rupert. Please lift him out of the pitfall of sidewalk living. Set his feet upon a rock and establish his steps. And protect him, letting no one lift his custom-fit shoes from the high-theft sidewalk where he sleeps. Amen.*

God's ways are far better than ours. If we trust in Him and acknowledge Him, He will direct our paths (Prov. 3:5–6). And if we make God and His kingdom our primary concern, He will supply everything we need, sometimes in unexpected ways. What a magnificent promise! Are you petitioning the sovereign King for your needs today?

> Seek first the kingdom of God and His righteousness,
> and all these things shall be added to you.
> [Give Him first place in your life, and He
> will meet your needs each day.]
> (Matt. 6:33)

THE KING'S LOVE LANGUAGE

Dr. Gary Chapman's popular book series on the five love languages presents ways to effectively communicate our love to someone who may speak a different love language than we do.

The idea is that each person has a primary love language that speaks the most meaningfully to him or her. An individual's preference could be: (1) words of affirmation, (2) quality time, (3) receiving gifts, (4) acts of service, or (5) physical touch. If we identify someone's primary love language and speak it rather than our own (which is our natural tendency), our loved one can better receive our affections.

Exploring this concept in light of Scripture, Dr. Chapman says that God speaks to us using all five of these methods, and we can speak all five to Him as well.[27] Going one step further, I suggest there's an even more meaningful love language we could speak to *Our Matchless King,* one that will lead to untold blessings.

Jesus told us this fundamental truth: "If anyone loves Me, he will keep My word" (John 14:23). Hence, the Lord's primary love language is our obedience to His word. By making moment-by-moment choices to do things God's way instead of our own, especially when facing strong fleshly temptations, we will effectively express our heart of worship to Him.

Our obedient choices bless our King as crowns of love if our motive is love instead of duty (see 1 John 4:19). Such crowns convey our surrendered hearts, declaring our allegiance to our awesom-azing God.

The Holy Spirit will empower believers to obey God's instructions if we yield to Him rather than to the desires of our flesh (Gal. 5:16; Phil. 4:13). And when we make choices to please God, He will bless us with more revelations of His truth. Oswald Chambers explains this great concept in his devotional on Matthew 11:25:

> Obey God in the thing [biblical truth] He shows you, and instantly the next thing is opened up. One reads [volumes of books] on the work of the Holy Spirit, when five minutes of drastic obedience would make things as clear as a sunbeam.[28]

Would you like to speak to *Our Matchless King* using His primary love language? You will have countless opportunities to do so. Take for example Jesus' instruction to love one another as He has loved us (John 13:34–35). Is there someone at work whom you struggle to love? Why not place that relationship on God's altar as a love offering (see Matt. 16:24)? Then ask God's Spirit to empower you to display His sacrificial love to him or her.

If you do, others will know you are Jesus' disciple, you will be proclaiming His worthiness, and you will be presenting the King with the highest heavenly treasure—a gift indeed fit for royalty.

> Has the Lord as great delight in burnt offerings
> and sacrifices, as in obeying the voice of the
> Lord? Behold, to obey is better than sacrifice.
> (1 Sam. 15:22)

KING OF KINGS
AND LORD OF LORDS

On the desolate island of Patmos, John (the last living apostle) saw a vision of Jesus Christ while "in the Spirit on the Lord's Day" (Rev. 1:10). John then wrote the book of Revelation under the inspiration of the Holy Spirit.

Toward the end of this apocalyptic book, we read a description of our soon-returning Lord of lords (19:11–16). Riding a white horse and wearing many crowns, He will come back to earth to reign over the nations with all power and authority.

Although Jesus was the Suffering Servant at His first coming, He will be the Conquering King at His second coming. The Lamb of God, who was sacrificed and broken for us, will come back triumphant as the Lion of the tribe of Judah.

One popular radio pastor powerfully contrasts these two paradoxical aspects of His character:

> The first time Jesus came, He allowed Himself to be mocked on our behalf; but the second time, He will majestically return and nothing He declared will ever be mocked. The first time He came powerless as a baby born in a manger; but He will return in all the power of heaven. The first time He came as a Lamb, and the second time He will come as a Lion. The first time He came to serve, but the second time He will come to *be* served. The first time He came to save us, the second time He will come to sovereignly rule.[29]

Hallelujah! Our risen Savior—the King of kings—is coming back with all authority "to judge the earth, to remake it, and to rule it in righteousness."[30]

Did you know that you are enrolled in the Lord's army? When He returns, He will lead an innumerable army of saints, comprised of all true believers, riding on white horses. But none of us will be harmed in the great battle in the Megiddo Valley. In fact, one word from our King's lips will take down all the enemy troops (19:21).

Aren't you grateful that God has given us a preview of future events and that you're on the winning team? Although Jesus twice said, "I am coming quickly!" (see 22:7, 20), there is still time for more trusting souls to enlist. As we wait expectantly for His return, we can broadcast this news flash: the ultimate battle belongs to the coming King, He wants to have a loving relationship with every person, and He wants to give each of us a set of keys to enter His matchless kingdom.

> His eyes were like a flame of fire, and on His head were
> many crowns…He was clothed with a robe dipped in blood,
> and His name is called The Word of God…Out of His mouth
> goes a sharp sword, that with it He should strike the nations.
> And He Himself will rule them with a rod of iron.
> He Himself treads the winepress of the fierceness and
> wrath of Almighty God. And He has on His robe
> and on His thigh a name written:
> KING OF KINGS AND LORD OF LORDS.
> (Rev. 19:12–16)

A splash of apologetics to share

FULFILLED MESSIANIC PROPHECIES

The credentials of Jesus as the Messiah are authenticated by Bible prophecy. Jesus fulfilled three hundred messianic prophecies from the Old Testament when He came to earth in the first century AD—sixty-one of which were major messianic prophecies.[31]

Here is just one example. The prophet Micah predicted in the eighth century BC that the Messiah would be born in Bethlehem (Micah 5:2).

> And indeed, that village was the very location of Jesus' birth (see Matt. 2:1–6; John 7:42). Other predictive prophecies pertained to His life, death, resurrection, and everlasting rule.
>
> The statistical probability of any one man fulfilling just eight such prophecies is 1 in 10^{17} (1 in 100,000,000,000,000,000). The chance of any one man fulfilling forty-eight of them is 1 in 10^{157}.[32] Jesus' identity as the Messiah has been firmly established.
>
> (For an overview of prophecies fulfilled by Jesus Christ, see the endnote.[33])

RAMPING UP OUR PRAYER LIFE

When was the last time you ran into the throne room to exercise your prayer rights as a son or daughter of the Most High? Was it today, or yesterday, or has it been a while?

Pastor Bob Botsford phrased this question another way. "Have you drifted in your prayer life so that the Lion who dwells in you has fallen asleep?"[34] Jesus Christ, the Lion of the tribe of Judah, resides in us by the Holy Spirit. He is ready, willing, and able to work wonders in and through His children if we stay plugged into the Power Source.

Pastor Botsford went on to say:

> If you haven't been praying, then chances are you haven't heard [the Lion] roar in a long, long time. It's like the Lion is asleep. It's like He's hibernating somewhere deep down in the den of your soul and you don't even know how to get down there anymore—'cause it's all about the fashionable things up on the surface. And yet He's there, and He waits, and He wants so much to be heard.[35]

The King's scepter is extended even now, warmly inviting you to approach Him in prayer. It may seem like *Our Matchless King* has to "take time from running the universe" (to use Rupert's expression) to hear your prayers and lavish His love on you. However, you will never have to "time-share" His attention.[36] The One who loved you and gave Himself for you (Gal. 2:20) promises to remain with you and treat you royally.

Why not ramp up your prayer time with the Lion of the tribe of Judah right now? Decide to draw nearer to Him and experience His glorious presence. Dialogue with Him throughout the day. And consider ways to set aside undisturbed time for your Scripture reading so you can familiarize yourself with His majesty and truth. Then your King and Best Friend can counsel and guide you, give you strength and comfort when needed, and bless your day with perspective and joy.

Let's enter His gates with thanksgiving and enter His courts with praise (Ps. 100:4). When we begin to worship the Worthy One, rejoicing in His goodness, we will soon hear Him roar! For the King of glory—who won the crowning victory at the cross of Calvary—dwells with us and makes His home in our worship (Ps. 22:3).[37]

> Who is this King of glory? The Lord strong and
> mighty; the Lord mighty in battle. Lift up your heads,
> O you gates! And lift them up, you everlasting
> doors! And the King of glory shall come in…
> The Lord of hosts, He is the King of glory.
> (Ps. 24:8–10)

WORSHIPPING GOD FOR HIS AWESOM-AZING ATTRIBUTES

He is sovereign, and He is/has majesty and eternality.

Dear King of heaven, I enter Your gates with thanksgiving and enter Your courts with praise. For you are the eternal God, who sovereignly rules the universe. I marvel at Your majesty and goodness. Thank You for treating me as Your royal son or daughter and joint heir to the throne with Christ. I pray that Your Holy Spirit will help me to be a loyal subject of Yours—to honor You and bring You glory. Thank You for the privilege to know You, draw near to You, and praise You endlessly. In Jesus' miraculous name, amen.

THE GOD WHO'S THERE

DWELLS WITHIN US AND NEVER LEAVES

For [God] Himself has said,
"I will never leave you nor forsake you."
So we may boldly say: "The Lord is my helper;
I will not fear. What can [mere] man do to me?"
(Heb. 13:5–6)

NAILS IN THE UNDERGROUND STORAGE SPACE

"OH, LORD, PLEASE don't let me step on a nail down here," I called out as I swept my straw broom across the cement floor of our underground crawl space. My husband had accepted a two-year job out of state, and I stayed behind a few days to clean up our home for renters. Our packers from the van lines had gone home, and the setting sun provided just enough light through the window to complete one last project for the day.

Dust flew around my designated dirt piles, forming a paste from the sweat on my face.

My aching, hunched-over back longed to complete my sweeping task so I could exit the cubbyhole and unwind my vertebrae without bumping my head on a rafter.

Barefoot and blinking, I swept faster as the outdoor light began to dim. Then I spotted some precariously placed construction nails—some lying loose on the cement floor, others protruding from wooden two-by-fours. Home alone, I certainly didn't need a medical emergency. Yet I didn't want to crawl out the miniature doorway to fetch my shoes. And the reward of a nice hot bath spurred me on. So I proceeded cautiously and shot up to heaven a one-sentence "arrow prayer" for protection.

As I took my next step, a three-inch nail came right up through my foot. "Yikes!" I yelped and froze in place. I stared at my foot in amazement, wondering why I felt no pain and saw no blood. Then I realized that the nail had wedged between two toes. It hadn't even broken my skin.

Wow! Thank You, Lord. I wasn't wounded at all! God had answered my arrow prayer. Maneuvering my dustpan and measuring my footsteps, I swept my dirt piles into a plastic trash bag. Then I exited unscathed from the mine field and headed for my hot bath.

As I wiped the mud pack off my face, I reflected on the nail incident, wondering if there was a spiritual application there. The Lord spoke these words to my heart: *You don't have to bear the pain of a nail through your foot; I've already done that for you.*

With blurry eyes filled with adoration, I thought about Jesus' sacrificial love for me. The nail that pierced His feet was no mere three-inch construction nail but a stake seven to nine inches long. I thanked Him for being my Deliverer and the Shield around me.

I hadn't been alone in that storage space after all. The Lord assures His redeemed, "I will never leave you nor forsake you" (Heb. 13:5). That Scripture, I discovered, contains not one but five negatives, meaning "I will never, never, never, never, never leave you nor forsake you."[38]

And because God's character is trustworthy and unchanging (Mal. 3:6), we know He won't depart from us even for a second— no matter how alone we may seem at times.

If you are living in communion with the Lord of heaven, when troubles and trials come your way He will guard you, hold your hand, and carry you through. He promises to be with you through thick and thin. In view of His personal nearness, why not allow His unfailing love to sweep your heart into deeper devotion to Him? Then you'll be able to depend on Him with *thicker* faith and *thinner* delay.

> He who dwells in the secret place of
> the Most High shall abide under the shadow
> of the Almighty. I will say of the Lord,
> "He is my refuge and my fortress;
> my God, in Him I will trust."
> (Ps. 91:1–2)

TURNING PAGES OF A NEW CHAPTER

One week after my nail-through-the-foot incident, I wrapped things up for our out-of-state move and boarded a midnight flight to meet my husband in Indiana. I collapsed into my airplane seat—exhausted yet relieved. Tears trickled down my cheek as I thought about leaving family and friends behind. I imagined the culture shock I'd experience while turning the pages of a new chapter of my life, where the action, plot, and characters would be vastly different and totally unpredictable.

As insecurity tried to tempt me, I started to wonder: *Will God be with me in the Midwest? Is He really guiding my life?* Then the Holy Spirit brought to my mind one of my life verses from the Bible: "Trust in the Lord with all your heart, and lean not on your own understanding. In all your ways acknowledge Him, and He shall direct your paths" (Prov. 3:5–6).

Yes, surely God would be with me. He would direct my path, and my husband's path too, because we were trusting in Him and seeking His will for our lives. And there wasn't anywhere on the face of the earth I'd rather be than in the center of His will. I smiled with reassurance as I recalled the precise positioning of that dreadful nail between my toes.

I reclined my airplane seat, put on my headset, and turned on my CD player. As I closed my eyes, a marvelous melody began to play and a vocalist began to sing: "The nails in Your hands, the nail in Your feet, they tell me how much You love me."[39]

Oh, my goodness! Confirmation of God's personal love flooded my heart with joy and peace. Although I had no idea why God was moving us to a state far away from family, I longed to broadcast in Indiana the message of Jesus' love for everyone. I prayed for Spirit-led words and actions.

How many times has the Lord overwhelmed your heart by reminding you of His loving presence and His guidance? How did you respond? Maybe you, too, wanted to broadcast the ultimate love message that Jesus Christ—God Almighty in the flesh—stepped down from the glories of heaven to redeem us (Phil. 2:5–11).

If you've never felt God's love strongly, ask Him right now to confirm it to your heart. Perhaps read John 3:16 aloud, inserting your first name in the verse:

> *For God so loved _________________ that He gave His only begotten Son, that whoever believes in Him should not perish but have everlasting life.*

Then consider sharing that passage with someone, filling in his or her name. With its inherent power, that revelation will convey the truth that God's love can set them free. As demonstrated on the cross, His love is extreme…unsurpassable…purely divine…and ever-present!

Behold, the virgin shall be with child, and bear a Son
[Jesus], and they shall call His name Immanuel,
which is translated, "God with us."
(Matt. 1:23)

JEHOVAH-SHAMMAH IS WITH US

Have you ever cried out in desperation, *God, are You really there?*
One of God's most exciting and powerful names is Jehovah-
Shammah, or *The God Who's There.* His name assures us that He
is right here with us (see Acts 17:28). Even pronouncing that
Hebrew name phonetically (*yeh-ho-vaw' shawm'-maw*)[40] sounds
powerful, doesn't it?

In the final verse of the book of Ezekiel, God gave a magnificent promise to the children of Israel. He would live among them
during the millennium (the future thousand-year reign of Christ
on earth).[41] He inspired them after their seventy years of captivity in Babylon by declaring that the restored and beautiful city of
Jerusalem would be named Jehovah-Shammah, translated as "*The
Lord Is There*" (Eze. 48:35). During that kingdom age, God's name
will be inseparably linked with His chosen city.[42] And thankfully,
all believers will dwell there with the Messiah, sharing His reign
in peace and righteousness (see Rev. 5:10; 20:4).

In one sense, God is present with everyone, because one of
His attributes is omnipresence. As the psalmist wrote, "Where
can I go from Your Spirit? Or where can I flee from your presence?" (Ps. 139:7). The Creator and Sustainer of the universe is
everywhere and holds all things together (Col. 1:17; Heb. 1:3).[43]

As believers, however, we have an added bonus: the Holy
Spirit resides within us. Thus, we can communicate with Jehovah-
Shammah at any time! (See Rom. 8:11; 1 Cor. 3:16.)

When my granddaughter Jenna was nine years old, she captured the joy of knowing that Jesus is always with her by writing
a poem. Here are some of the lyrics (with her own spelling):

Jesus, I know You're there, down deep in my heart. I believe You're the Saver of the world. You make me smile. You make me happie. Jesus, U R the Saver of the world. I love U…and I always will.

The "Saver" of the world is preparing a place for us to live with Him in heavenly mansions (John 14:2). In light of our future, let's make the most of every day. Why not allow the Potter to soften your clay daily with a few drops of living water from His Word? As He forms you into a vessel of honor, other clay vessels might observe His reflection in you, or overhear you speak of the Master, and eventually come alive themselves. Then Christ—the only hope of glory—will also dwell with them.

> God willed to make known what are the riches
> of the glory of this mystery among the Gentiles:
> which is Christ [living] in you, the hope of glory.
> (Col. 1:27)

AN UNEXPECTED SCHOLARSHIP

Despite having no income and still sleeping in the homeless camp after two months, my friend Rupert displayed what my husband calls moxie. Every day he rose early (so as not to get ticketed for illegal lodging), then packed up his possessions, ate breakfast at the shelter, and headed to the library to send out resumes that he and I had prepared on my computer.

Through our ongoing e-mails, I noticed that Rupert had exceptional communication skills and used lively metaphors. Eager to help my friend, I encouraged him to write a few short devotionals from the perspective of his struggles on the sidewalks of San Diego, and he did.

His first three devotionals promised to bless the socks off most anyone. When I realized what a gifted writer he was, I wondered if pursuing a writing career might be the avenue God was lining out for him. Perhaps he could benefit by attending the writers' conference I already had in my schedule. The speakers and work-shops could help sharpen his skills and clarify God's plans for him. It might also give him a boost of encouragement.

There were only two days left to register for the event. "Lord," I prayed, "I'm placing a fleece before You, kind of like Gideon did. I'll apply for a scholarship on Rupert's behalf and submit it with a sample of his writing. If You want him to attend the conference with me, please open that door for him."

Although the full scholarships were already granted, Rupert qualified for a partial one. So I launched an e-mail to my friends, attaching one of his "Devos from the Sidewalks of Santee." Within a few hours, several pledges of support came in—amazingly, in the exact amount required: $125.00.

During the event, faculty members and fellow conferees affirmed his exceptional writing ability. Although he felt a bit overwhelmed, he learned techniques and made contacts. Jehovah-Shammah, *The God Who's There*, was definitely with Rupert at the conference.

Our loving God says that His plans for us are for a good future and full of hope (Jer. 29:11). And since He is always with us, His cherished thoughts are upon us continuously. Doesn't that concept seem too glorious to assimilate? It did to David the psalmist (Ps. 139:1–10). He described God's thoughts toward us as greater in number than all the grains of sand…on all the beaches…in all the world (v. 18).

Thank You, Lord, for Your countless thoughts toward us and Your unexpected blessings, such as the victories You bring in the middle of our battles. From Your complete macro view, You see the big picture from every angle, then minister to each of us personally. I rejoice in Your goodness. In Jesus' name, amen.

How precious also are Your thoughts to me,
O God! How great is the sum of them! If I
should count them, they would be more in number
than the sand; when I awake, I am still with You.
(Ps. 139:17–18)

A splash of apologetics to share

PASCAL'S WAGER: A LOGICAL APPEAL TO ATHEISTS

Blaise Pascal, a seventeenth-century French mathematical genius, posed this hypothetical question: What happens when we die, according to atheism and theism?

If there is no God, there's no payoff at the end, whether we wager for or against the existence of God. For we neither gain nor lose anything if we do not exist.

But if there is a God, the wager to believe in Him (and make peace with Him during our lifetime) offers us an infinite payoff—eternal life in joy with God!

Thus, atheism is a no-win bet. Faith is a no-lose bet.[44]

* * *

God promises that if we will search for Him with all our hearts, we will find Him (Jer. 29:13). He will reveal Himself to seekers (Acts 8:26–40). He will reward those who diligently seek Him (Heb. 11:6). And joy and purpose will replace any sense of hopelessness or insignificance.

Christians can attest to these truths experientially because *The God Who's There* resides within them permanently (Rom. 8:11) and confirms deep in their hearts that they are children of the living God (v. 16).

MY CONSTANT COMPANION

During the peak traffic hour in Southern California one day, I drove my car up an on-ramp and entered Interstate 5. As soon as I merged into the slow lane, I heard a loud bang. Then my car swerved out of control, heading left across four lanes.

As my world whirled around me, I closed my eyes and cried out, "Jesus!"

My Camry hit the center divider of the freeway, then landed safely in a dirt shoulder. Just twenty feet beyond me, the shoulder ended abruptly. Whew! Only the Lord knows how many cars would have plowed into me from behind if there hadn't been that timely niche of escape.

When I realized God had miraculously spared my life, I immediately thanked Him for being "Johnny on the spot." However, after gathering my wits, I apologized for my short-sighted remark. The Alpha and Omega—who knows the end from the beginning—didn't instantly show up to rescue me! Nothing catches Him by surprise. Instead, I praised Him for being my Constant Companion.

As I sat trapped in my car, trembling like a leaf, a highway patrolman arrived and assessed the situation. "You're a very fortunate lady," he remarked. "Look at your skid marks across those lanes. And you're not even injured?"

"Oh, I know why I wasn't hurt," I replied. "At the exact moment my car started swerving, I called on the name of Jesus."

The officer smiled and gave me a thumbs-up. "I know what you mean!"

Based on the placement of the dents in my car, the patrolman determined that a large truck had hit my rear fender. He called for roadside assistance, and within an hour, my car was towed to a gas station. I surprised myself by boldly declaring to six people there that God had just saved my life in a freeway accident. "So remember to call on the powerful name of Jesus," I pleaded with them.

You never know whom God might place in your pathway who's ripe to hear a passionate testimony about *The God Who's There*. I prayed on that traumatic day that the Holy Spirit would speak to hearts through my words. For our awesom-azing God will respond to anyone who calls on the name of Jesus (Rom. 10:13).

Perhaps you can recall a crisis in your own life when you cried out to Jesus and He intervened. Why not share that victory in Christ with others? It will encourage the brethren. And you could point out to pre-Christians that the greatest disaster they could ever face is their separation from God. But if they call on our Redeemer, trusting in Him, He will welcome them into His family and be their Constant Companion—today, tomorrow, and forever.

> He shall call upon Me, and I will answer
> him; I will be with him in trouble;
> I will deliver him and honor him.
> (Ps. 91:15)

PRAYING FOR THE MIND OF CHRIST

With fragmented thoughts, I slammed down the phone. I'd just been told that my seven-year-old grandson, Nicky, was scheduled to have emergency ear surgery. After discussing the matter with my husband, I booked a flight to Colorado to assist my son's family.

As my airplane flew over snowy alpine peaks, I asked the Lord how He wanted me to help out. At that instant, an image of the Lord's forehead flashed before my eyes. Dark wavy hair parted down the middle framed His forehead. Struck with amazement at the vision He blessed me with, I wondered what it meant.

Later that day, at the children's hospital, I caught up with Nicky, who was clothed in a powder-blue checkered gown and clutching a small stuffed monkey. After passing out hugs to my grandson and his parents, I followed them down the hall for Nicky's MRI scan.

At my earliest opportunity, I phoned my prayer partner, Joanie, in California. I told her about the supernatural vision I had on the plane, and the Lord graciously gave her the interpretation: He wanted me to humbly seek the "mind of Christ" (to discern His will) throughout my stay (see 1 Cor. 2:16).

I took this message to heart, welcoming the confirmation that Jehovah-Shammah was with me, and I was on board with Him. I considered it my temporary calling, as Nicky's Nana, to consider God's perspective when praying. During each challenge or critical moment, I asked the Holy Spirit to help me stay humble (Phil. 2:3–5) and inspire my prayers so they'd line up with God's plan (1 John 5:14–15).

Nicky's critical surgery was successful. All glory to God! The infection behind his ear had traveled up to the lining of the brain, but didn't go inside. After several days of testing and treatment, he was released to go home.

When I returned home, I decided to ask the Lord every day to give me a greater measure of His Holy Spirit, knowing that our heavenly Father delights in answering that petition (Luke 11:13).

What a mighty and merciful God we serve! His Holy Spirit imparts spiritual discernment to us so we can pray with His empowerment, speak His truth, understand His Scripture, and thereby accomplish great things.

A few weeks later, my daughter-in-law phoned me with an update. After several days of follow-up home care, Nicky was feeling fine and had returned to school. Of course, that didn't mean Nana could get off her knees and stop praying for him. But right then, I danced the "Nana Shuffle" across my kitchen floor, praising God.

Since the big-picture purpose of prayer is to get heaven's will done on earth, rather than to get our will done in heaven, let's seek (a portion of) the mind of Christ when lifting up our petitions. If we do, we will surely see more answers to our prayers. And the ramifications in heaven, as well as on earth, could be endless.

If we ask anything according to His will, He
hears us. And if we know that He hears us,
whatever we ask, we know that we have the
petitions that we have asked of Him.
(1 John 5:14–15)

A splash of apologetics to share

GOD'S SUPREME REVELATION OF HIMSELF

We can know that God exists primarily because He revealed Himself to us through His Son. The Bible teaches that Jesus Christ is the express image of the invisible God, and in Jesus dwells all the fullness of God in bodily form (Col. 1:15; 2:9).

Jesus of Nazareth Himself made the radical claim that He was eternal God who came to earth in human form (John 8:58; 14:9). His claim was validated by:

- His performance of numerous miracles

- His fulfillment of extensive Bible prophecy

- His supernatural resurrection from the dead.

According to the New Testament (a compilation of reliable primary-source, first-century documents[45]), Jesus was unique in His pre-birth announcements, birth, life, death, and resurrection. He was born of a virgin; He was sinless; He was crucified and buried, but He returned to life on the third day.

(For an overview of evidence for the existence of God, see the endnote.[46])

THE BRIDGE BETWEEN HEAVEN AND EARTH

Jacob ran for his life, fleeing from his angry brother Esau, whom he had deceived. (Perhaps you're familiar with that story, presented in Genesis 27.) Finally exhausted, he stopped at sundown to camp. Using a rock for a pillow, he lay down and fell asleep (Gen. 28:11).

In a divinely inspired dream, Jacob saw a ladder extending from earth to heaven, with angels traveling up and down it. We discover in the New Testament that this ladder represented Jesus Christ—the bridge between heaven and earth (John 1:47–51).

In this life-changing dream, the Lord appeared above the ladder and said, "I am the Lord." He then gave Jacob the same covenant promises He had given to his grandfather Abraham, followed by four personal promises: I am with you, I will protect you wherever you go, I will bring you back to this land, and I will fulfill My plans in your life (Gen. 28:15).

When Jacob woke up, he realized that Jehovah-Shammah was with him personally. He exclaimed, "Surely the Lord is in this place, and I did not know it" (v. 16). He had assumed, based on a limited view of God, that by running away from home, he was also running away from God.[47]

When Jacob arose, he took the stone from under his head and set it upright as a memorial pillar, then anointed it with oil to become a place for worship. He renamed the city Bethel, meaning "House of God." And he made a sacred vow: the Lord would be his God (vv. 18–22).

When we are stuck in fearful or rocky situations, such as a difficult marriage, an unsatisfactory job, or financial troubles, the Lord likewise promises us, "I am with you in this place, even though you may not know it." Then we have a decision to make. Will we acknowledge His presence, seek Him, and try to fit into His plan? Or will we disregard Him and handle the situation in our own way?

May we remember that *The God Who's There*, who desires to fulfill His plans in our lives, has bridged heaven and earth for each of us. And He did so at such great personal expense—to reconcile us to Himself, to show us His closeness, and to display His infinite love for us. So why not ask Him to draw you nearer? He's there even when you lay your head down on your pillow at night. You might also ask Him to give you sweet dreams and sound sleep. Or even divinely inspired dreams—after all, God works the night shift too.

> God demonstrates His own love toward us, in
> that while we were still sinners, Christ [our
> Bridge] died for us…We were reconciled
> to God through the death of His Son.
> (Rom. 5:8–10)

NYQUIL TABS ON THE SIDEWALK

After Rupert's writers' conference, he returned to "Hellapalooza Corner" (his name for the sidewalk) to wait his turn for a bed at the homeless shelter. As I had dreaded, he faced another round of devastating circumstances.

First, a respectable guy in the homeless camp, whom Rupert had befriended, died from a sudden heart attack. Then, after Rupert carefully submitted four of his devotionals online to a magazine, the website field boxes deleted them all. After that, he got sick with the flu. Spiritual warfare and prolonged sidewalk living continued to beat him down.

However, Rupert's status as a King's kid afforded him certain inalienable rights—namely, God's sovereign watch over his life (John 10:28–29).

A few days after he recovered from the flu, my concern for him turned to hope when I received another e-mail. Here is an excerpt:

Earlier this week I met an articulate black guy named Wes. He said he appreciated talking to me because I don't come out with all that stuff of the street. When he said I was refreshing and intelligent, I just scratched my head and thanked him. He told me his story and why he always has a smile. It's because he used to be one of those crack heads, and now he's a vital, healthy, positive dude—homeless, but saved. It picked up my spirits.

Then the flu virus knocked me back down again. But God put some Nyquil tabs on the sidewalk—two for daytime and two for nighttime. I don't know where they came from, but they helped me get back on my feet. I still hack a lot, but at least I can get around.

I wondered whether Wes was a ministering angel dispatched by God to help my friend recover from the flu. If so, on his way to Hellapalooza Corner, he probably stopped at the Divine Pharmacy to pick up four Nyquil tabs!

Do you look for God in the little things in your life? He cares about the details of our lives, and He knows our every need in advance. Our part is to petition Him through our prayers, knowing that His ways and thoughts are higher than ours (Isa. 55:9).

Jesus told us to expect trouble and tribulation here on earth, but assured us that He has overcome this world (John 16:33). As we wait for Jesus to enforce His grand victory on the cross, let's keep calling on Him in times of need. Since we are kids of the King, He is sovereign over our circumstances, and He will make a way for us through the clutter and clamor of this fallen world.

> The Lord [Jehovah-Shammah] is near
> to all who call upon Him, to all
> who call upon Him in truth.
> (Ps. 145:18)

JOLENE AND JEHOVAH-SHAMMAH

Jolene decided years ago she'd no longer try to convince her husband, Jim, to become a believer. That was the job of the Holy Spirit.

One day Jim was nervously pacing around the house. Finally she said, "Jim, you'd better tell me what's wrong or you'll need to go see a doctor!"

He paused for a minute, then explained. "We've been so desperate financially that I withdrew twenty thousand dollars out of our 401(k) and placed it in speculative stocks that could yield a lot of money in just three weeks. But it didn't succeed. It collapsed."

Instead of getting angry with Jim, or reminding him that he had promised never to participate in high-risk money ventures again, Jolene responded from her heart. She had spent devotional time with the Lord that morning meditating on His Word, and she was filled with a supernatural calmness (see John 14:27).

She said, "You know what, honey? The Enemy of our souls comes to rob, kill, and destroy, but I'm not going to let him rob me of my peace, even though we're in financial turmoil. The Lord gives me joy and peace even in times of trouble. We'll get through this somehow."

I suspect Jolene's gentle yet powerful witness of our awesomazing God impressed Jim, don't you? Despite their escalating financial crisis, she didn't get ruffled, panicked, or accusatory. By walking in the Spirit and not gratifying the flesh (Gal. 5:16), she gave the Enemy no opening to instigate an argument or diminish her contentment. She even splashed out living water toward Jim by sharing the truth of God's Word (the John 10:10 passage) with a loving attitude.

Considering God's continual presence with us, author Francis Chan writes, "May we learn to pray for an open and willing heart, to surrender to the Spirit's leading with that friend, child, spouse, circumstance, or decision in our lives right now."[48] If we do, we will honor God and impact others' lives for Christ. (See John 15:5.)

By yielding to the Holy Spirit, Jolene demonstrated to Jim that she had more than a religion. She displayed what it looks like to walk with Jesus in a dynamic relationship. *The God Who's There* inspired her words, thoughts, and actions—promising to yield high returns in her marriage and in her Christian witness.

Do you want people to see Jesus in you? If so, converse with the Lord and dwell on His Word each day. If you start to drift in your devotional time, pray for an increased hunger for fellowship with Him and an increased thirst for the living water of Scripture. Then chances are, you will face any turmoil in your day with the kind of calmness that leads others to take note of Who you spend time with.

> When they saw the [Christ-confidence]
> of Peter and John,…they realized that
> they had been with Jesus.
> (Acts 4:13)

"I WILL BE WITH YOU."

Jehovah-Shammah is with us when we answer our e-mails, when we go shopping, when we negotiate a business deal, when we eat dinner, or when we feed the baby. He stays with His sons and daughters always. Even during times of hardship when God seems distant—or when friends, family, or the brethren forsake you—the Lord will not depart. And someday when we get the whole story, we will see that "yes indeed, God was there directing the situation the entire time."[49]

Check out some of these assurances that our devoted, relational God made to His people:

- The Lord told Isaac, "I will be with you." (Gen. 26:3)

- The Lord told Jacob, "I will be with you." (Gen. 31:3)

- The Lord told Moses, "I will certainly be with you." (Ex. 3:12)

- The Lord told Joshua, "I will be with you." (Josh. 1:5; 3:7)
- The Lord told Gideon, "I will be with you." (Judg. 6:16)
- The Lord told Jeroboam, "I will be with you." (1 Kings 11:38)
- The Lord told Israel, "I will be with you." (Isa. 43:2)
- The Lord told Zerubbabel, "I am with you." (Hag. 2:4)
- The Lord told David, "I have been with you." (2 Sam. 7:9)
- The Lord told Jeremiah, "I am with you." (Jer. 1:8, 19; 15:20)
- Jesus told the apostle Paul, "I am with you." (Acts 18:10)
- Jesus told His disciples (then and now), "I am with you always." (Matt. 28:20)

One way to experience the Lord's presence is through worship, for He makes Himself at home in the praises of His people (Ps. 22:3). One Bible teacher wrote this about coming before God with a praise-filled heart: "It brings Him to me. Or perhaps it takes me to Him."[50] Heartfelt worship of God also chases away the Enemy and bring us victories (see 2 Chron. 20:21–22; Acts 16:25–26).

Does knowing that God loves you—and that He will never, never, never, never, never leave you or forsake you—motivate you to deepen your devotional life with Him? His nearness will bring you peace and joy (Ps. 16:11). You will appreciate more deeply that nothing can separate you from Him or from His love (Rom. 8:1, 38–39).[51] And He will help you…and strengthen you…and sustain you.

> Fear not, for I am with you;
> be not dismayed, for I am your God.
> I will strengthen you, yes, I will help you,
> I will uphold you with My righteous right hand.
> (Isa. 41:10)

Worshipping God for His Awesom-azing Attributes

He is omnipresent, and He is immutable.

Dear God, I praise You for Your continuous presence with me as The God Who's There. You will never let go of me, even for a second, because I belong to You. Since there's nowhere I could wander without Your Spirit joining me, I need not dread the darkness or fear any disconnection from You. That glorious truth enables me to forge ahead and serve You with gladness. With all my heart, I worship You for Your character, which is holy, trustworthy, majestic, unchangeable, and lacking in nothing. In Jesus' name, amen.

OUR DIVINE SYMPATHIZER

MINISTERS TO OUR DEEPEST NEEDS

*We do not have a High Priest who cannot sympathize
with our weaknesses…Let us therefore come boldly
to the throne of grace, that we may obtain mercy
and find grace to help in time of need.
(Heb. 4:15–16)*

A CALL IN TIME OF CRISIS

LORD, USE ME *as Your instrument in Janna's life today,* I prayed
while driving to the hospital emergency room. *Please don't let the
Enemy rip her off!*

Not many circumstances in life could cause me to drop everything and run. However, that morning I'd received an SOS phone
call from a sister in Christ. Her precious daughter Janna, whom
I had the pleasure of getting to know in a women's Bible study a
few years earlier, was borderline suicidal and wanted me to meet
her at the hospital.

After praying, I sensed God calling me to help out immediately. Since I'm not a licensed counselor, I knew I had to yield
fully to the Holy Spirit.

Before I took off for the ER, I typed a love letter addressed to Janna from the Lord—as if He were speaking to her in the crisis and assuring her of His everlasting love. The words poured through my fingers. I filled the letter with Scriptures I had heard on the radio that same morning, then added a border of colorful flowers. I concluded with this song refrain: "Turn your eyes upon Jesus. Look full in His wonderful face. And the things of earth will grow strangely dim, in the light of His glory and grace."[52]

After printing out the letter, I grabbed my Bible and ran out the door to join Janna and her mom in the ER lobby. The three of us stayed together during Janna's intensive intake interview. The triage nurse then recommended that she stay overnight for her protection on a psychiatric hold. Two medical assistants lifted her onto a gurney to transport her to another facility. There was no time for me to read Janna my letter. So I tucked the piece of paper under her sheet before they rolled her down the hallway.

A few weeks later, Janna filled me in. She had experienced a horrific night in the protection ward in the midst of troubled patients. But at one point during her distress, she rolled over in bed and discovered an envelope addressed to "Beloved Janna." Reading the contents over and over helped her to focus on Jesus instead of the fearful surroundings. The song lyrics blessed Janna in a special way because on the day before her emergency, her dad had encouraged her with the very same chorus: "Turn your eyes upon Jesus…"

Isn't our God awesom-azing? As *Our Divine Sympathizer,* He comforts us, relates to our weaknesses, and offers us grace and mercy (Heb. 4:15–16). He ministered to Janna's deep needs through His living Word and His presence with her.

We all go through storms in life. They're inevitable. The next time a crisis or emergency comes your way, call on the Lord for help with expectancy, and let His living Word serve as a healing balm over you. Be ready to turn your eyes upon Jesus…look full in His wonderful face…and occupy your thoughts with His glory, His grace, and your life with Him forever.

Set your mind on things above, not on things on the earth.
For you died [when Christ died], and your life is hidden
with Christ in God. When Christ who is our life
appears, then you also will appear with Him in glory.
(Col. 3:2–4)

KING DAVID RAN TO THE ROCK

God raised up David to be the king of Israel, *a man after God's own heart* who would do His will (Acts 13:22). Despite his failures, David prayed to the living God frequently and fervently. He penned psalms and prophecies, under the inspiration of the Holy Spirit. He expressed devotion and worship for his heavenly King. And he called on God in times of trouble.

When David felt boxed in or overwhelmed, he ran to his secret place of prayer for a "time out" (see Matt. 6:6). Consider a few of David's psalms that refer to our trustworthy God as a rock we can run to—in order to rethink, regroup, and regenerate.

- *In Psalm 18*, David praised the Lord for saving him from enemies that hotly pursued him. At any time, David could run to his rock, fortress, and deliverer (vv. 1–2).

- *In Psalm 32*, David exalted God for being his "hiding place." For He preserved David from trouble, surrounded him with victory songs, and instructed and guided him (vv. 7–8).

- *In Psalm 40*, David glorified God, who lifted him out of the horrible pit, set his "feet upon a rock," and established his steps (vv. 1–2).

- *In Psalm 61*, David thanked God for being his shelter and "strong tower from the enemy." And he asked Him to lead him to the rock whenever his heart grew faint (vv. 2–3).

- *In Psalm 62*, David declared that the Lord was his rock, and salvation, and defense. By faith, he could stand on solid spiritual ground and not be shaken (vv. 1–2).

Next time your heart is heavy and you need help or relief, follow David's pattern and run to God in prayer. From the vista at the rock of refuge, surely you will gain a higher point of view. There you will gain divine wisdom and enabling grace. After all, what better place could you go for counsel, deliverance, or comfort? He alone understands you fully, knows all things, loves you unfailingly, and always extends His arms of welcome.

Thank You, Lord Jesus, for being the Rock of my salvation and my place of refuge. Please help me today [describe your problems or vent your feelings]. I know You're reigning on the throne in heaven. Please also reign in my heart and over my circumstances. I can't wait to see what You'll do next in my situation. For You surely have a plan, and it is for good.

From the end of the earth I will cry to You,
when my heart is overwhelmed; lead me
to the rock that is higher than I.
(Ps. 61:2)

ENLIGHTENMENT AT CAMP "ID-RA-HA-JE"

Last summer at a week-long camp for kids in the Colorado mountains, my grandson surrendered his heart to Jesus Christ. I learned that thrilling news from Nicky himself. The name of his camp ("Id-Ra-Ha-Je") stands for *I'd Rather Have Jesus.*

On the final morning when the kids packed up to go home, Nicky's family (including me) drove up the mountain to meet him for breakfast and hear his reports. We enjoyed sausage and cinnamon rolls, then Nicky introduced us to his new friends and gave us a guided tour of the spacious grounds filled with fragrant pine trees.

One site was an A-frame shelter facing a large campfire pit, where Nicky had received Christ. The whole gang had gathered there for a powwow on the last night of the retreat. While seated around the fire pit, each kid shared one thing he or she had learned about God. With a beaming smile, Nicky told us his one-liner: "Even when people get seriously injured, God still has a plan."

Wow, his meaningful remark sounded similar to one I heard from a pastor when I was a brand-new believer. I had just resigned from a paralegal job due to persistent neck pain and headaches resulting from an auto accident. Soon afterward, I embarked upon a personal quest for meaning and truth in life, and a friend invited me to a women's Bible study at a non-denominational church. There I heard the gospel and became spiritually reborn.

When I met with the pastor to address my neck-pain issue, I asked him the age-old question "Why me?" With compassion in his voice, he replied, "I don't know, but sometimes God uses pain to turn our heads toward Him."[53]

His spiritual wisdom jolted me, opening my eyes to a bigger perspective. *Our Divine Sympathizer* had graciously allowed my pain to get my attention. Had I not changed courses in life, I'd be traveling down the wide road that leads to eternal destruction (Matt. 7:13–14). I began to praise God for permitting my physical ailments for a much higher cause.

I'd rather have Jesus (I love the title of that kids' camp!) than anything the world has to offer, even climbing a corporate ladder to worldly success. To be redeemed is surely worth any temporary heartbreak or humbling process.

How about praising God right now for bringing the gospel into your life, then translating you from the kingdom of darkness into the kingdom of the Son of His love (Col. 1:13)? As a result of His grace, someday you will live with Him in a joyous, pain-free environment…enjoying heavenly treasures that will never depreciate.

> What will it profit a man if he gains
> the whole world, and loses his
> own soul [in the process]?
> (Mark 8:36)

A splash of living water and apologetics

IF GOD IS LOVING AND ALL-POWERFUL, WHY DOES HE ALLOW PEOPLE TO SUFFER?

We are born into a world made chaotic
and unfair by a humanity in
revolt against its Creator.[54]

People who are unfamiliar with biblical revelation often assume that God is to blame for human suffering. What they fail to consider is that we are fallen people living in a fallen (broken) world. But such was not always the case. Originally, our loving God created the world and the people in it as perfect (see Gen. 1–3).

The problem: How did the human race fall? God gave our original ancestors free will. He gave Adam and Eve the capacity and freedom to accept or reject His love and to choose good or evil. God told Adam not to eat the fruit of one particular tree in the garden, and warned him that if he did he would die. But Eve, tempted by Satan, ate of the fruit. Adam followed her and ate also. At that point, sin and death entered the world and spread to all men. The human race became separated from God. (See Gen. 2:15–3:24; Rom. 5:12.)

The remedy: Holy justice had to be served for our rebellion. Yet we, as unrighteous people, were incapable of paying the debt. Astonishingly, God loved us so much that He decided to rescue and reclaim us by sending His own Son to die for our sins on the cross at Calvary (John 3:16). Our sinless Savior endured the greatest suffering known to mankind, both physically and spiritually, on our behalf (Matt. 27:29–50).[55]

The choice: As a result, whoever trusts in Jesus—who lived, died, and rose again—will live forever in God's glorious kingdom. That's the good news!

THE BEST IS YET TO COME

"God's chiseling hammer of love may sound like a paradox,"[56] stated Pastor Bob Botsford on his radio broadcast, "but His ways are far higher and better than ours." (See Isa. 55:9.)

Pastor Botsford went on to say that our trials and sufferings don't indicate that God has abandoned us. On the contrary, He goes with us through our trials, giving us grace. Our faith grows through hardships, and God wants us to become purified and come forth as gold. "The best is yet to come, when we see Jesus!"[57]

Remember Job's journey through intense suffering? Based on that account, one Bible commentator listed six lessons, or valuable benefits, associated with our trials and difficulties. They are summarized below:

- *Suffering prepares us for eternity.* God wants to develop our faith.

- *Satan is silenced by our submission to God's sovereignty.* When we worship God in times of suffering, instead of cursing or rebelling, He proves to the Enemy that He hasn't bought us off with blessings and ease.

- *Suffering produces a clearer vision of ourselves and God.* Going through deep waters allows us to view the Lord as more real and more precious. We will see more keenly our vileness and the Lord's holiness.

- *Suffering produces compassion.* Our own difficulties help us to gain compassion for others who are hurting and troubled. Then we can offer them real comfort.

- *Suffering teaches us humility.* After going through humbling hardships, we become less prideful and better able to receive revelations from the Lord.

- *Suffering has a happy ending.* The Lord takes us from glory to greater glory (2 Cor. 3:18) and from sorrow to unspeakable joy (John 16:20). When we reach heaven, we will be completely healed.[58]

Are you experiencing God's "chiseling hammer of love" in your life right now? If so, why not reread the benefits of suffering listed above, then live to please Jesus in anticipation of seeing Him. Such a life will indicate that you'd rather become more Christlike than more conformed to this world (see Rom. 12:2). And that you've personally encountered the living Lord…you've grasped a glimpse of His glory…and your eyes have opened to see that truly, *the best is yet to come!*

> But we all, with unveiled face [no longer with spiritual
> blinders], beholding as in a mirror the glory of the Lord,
> are being transformed into the same image from glory
> to glory [as the Spirit of the Lord works within us].
> (2 Cor. 3:18)

FACE-TO-FACE WITH A HEALTH CRISIS

"If you could say anything to Jesus right now, what would it be?" asked one of Sherrie's prayer sisters after a group luncheon.

Without hesitation, my friend replied, "Lord, Your will be done." Her heart soared with the truth of her words. She could finally trust God, regardless of the outcome.

Three years earlier, Sherrie was diagnosed with pulmonary fibrosis, a lung disease that makes people struggle to breathe. It produces scar tissue that steadily decreases airflow. Her doctor explained that the average life expectancy for people with this condition was three to five years.

At first, Sherrie lapsed into denial and unbelief. *Could there be a mistake? This can't be true! Maybe I should get a second opinion.* Her desperate thoughts and emotions took roller-coaster turns. She wasn't ready to depart from her family.

For a while, Sherrie shouldered the burden alone, only sharing her heartbreaking news with immediate family. She withdrew from everyday activities. Finally, unable to bear her struggles alone, Sherrie spoke to a pastor at her church.

After a few meetings together, he told her with tender sensitivity, "You have two choices, Sherrie. You can either hold a pity party, bringing all the attention to yourself. Or you can accept your condition and surrender it to the Lord, letting the attention go to Him. This illness is an opportunity for you to bring glory to God. You can grab that opportunity or let it slide by."

His advice was a major turning point for Sherrie. When she chose to focus on God's promises instead of her circumstances, He lifted her over the huge hurdle of acceptance. Sherrie decided to live for God's glory and entrust her health battle into His hands. Ultimately, as David declared to the Philistine giant, "the battle is the Lord's" (1 Sam. 17:47).

The Captain of Sherrie's ship guided her through the raging sea into still waters—extending her time with family and friends. Even while she battled the storms of adversity, she found purpose and contentment.

This passing world is filled with health and pain issues. If such things have come your way, why not surrender them to almighty God, treating them as opportunities to bring Him glory? If you embrace this truth for yourself, you will experience peace and fulfillment now, as well as God's richest blessings forever (2 Cor. 4:17). You will—as Anne Graham Lotz puts it—"live a life of eternal significance, intentionally."[59]

> Our light affliction, which is but for a moment
> [a brief time of trouble and suffering] is working
> for us a far more exceeding and eternal weight of glory.
> (2 Cor. 4:17)

GOD OF THE BIG PICTURE

After surrendering her health crisis to God, Sherrie faced another intense decision. Would she apply for a double lung transplant to prolong her life? She visited an intercessory group for prayer and scriptural wisdom, then decided to go forward with medical tests and appointments to see what God might have in store for her.

Doors began to open toward a transplant surgery. Yet it would be a long wait before she'd find out whether a suitable double lung would come along. Over time, her breathing equipment advanced from a portable canister with a small air tube, up to large R2D2-looking oxygen tanks delivered to her home weekly.

Various prayer chains, family members, and friends prayed consistently for "God's perfect match, in His perfect timing." My friend continued to ask the Lord for His will to be done, for His glory (1 Cor. 10:31).

Three years after being placed on the national transplant list, and with only a hint of airflow left, Sherrie's phone call came. "Praises to the God of the photo finish!" exclaimed her husband as he grabbed her suitcases to head for the hospital.

Sherrie received a double lung transplant that perfectly fit her small chest cavity. God guided her surgeon throughout the procedure. Loved ones prayed her through recovery. And eventually, my friend enjoyed walking around freely, no longer carting oxygen equipment.

When Sherrie returned to church, she related her victory in Christ to the parking lot attendant, who had reserved a handicap space for her car each Sunday morning. On another day, she made a special trip to the mall to share her miracle with a salesclerk she had befriended while breathing through an air tube. A short time later, she shared her exciting story with the pastor of a nearby church—the son of her own counseling pastor, whom God had used so mightily in her life.[60]

In an effort to encourage other people who face health crises, Sherrie wrote this message:

Trust in the God of the big picture. Seek Him, cling to His Word, and never give up. Invite Jesus into your crisis, asking for His will to be done for His glory. When doubts arise, cry out, "God, I have faith in You, but I need more!" If you turn your anxieties into prayers, earnestly and with thanksgiving (Phil. 4:6–7), He'll calm your heart because you live in His heart.[61]

Our magnificent Lord, whose nature is pure love and goodness, is worthy to receive glory and honor (Rev. 4:11). He avails Himself to us as *Our Divine Sympathizer*, ready to minister to our deepest personal needs.

In light of that glorious truth, why not wrap your arms around Him, embracing Him in worship and thanksgiving? Then turn your anxieties into prayers, trusting in the God of the Big Picture, as Sherrie did. If you do, chances are you will find yourself joyfully passing on your own personal testimonies about His wondrous ways.

> Whether you eat or drink, or whatever
> you do, do all to the glory of God.
> (1 Cor. 10:31)

Splashes of living water

TEN LIFELINES TO CLING TO WHEN STORMS HIT HOME

These biblical actions will enable believers to find peace and purpose in any adversity or struggle.[62]

1. Meditate on God's living Word (Heb. 4:12).

2. Develop your prayer life (Phil. 3:10; 1 Thess. 5:17).

3. Mature in your Christian faith (1 Peter 1:7).

> 4. Share your personal testimonies (Matt. 5:16).
>
> 5. Minister to others in need (Mark 9:35).
>
> 6. Show appreciation to loved ones (John 15:12).
>
> 7. Wear the armor of God daily (Eph. 6:10–18).
>
> 8. Praise and worship the Lord (Rev. 4:11).
>
> 9. Maintain a humble and grateful heart (Eph. 4:32).
>
> 10. Abide in the Lord, making your home in Him through unbroken fellowship (John 15:7).

MOTIVATED BY CHRIST'S LOVE

Paul the apostle encountered perils nearly everywhere he went. More than once he came within an inch of his life in his efforts to preach the gospel. His life's passion was to know Christ, to become like Christ, and to be all that Christ had in mind for him (Phil. 3:10). He lived to please God rather than man.

When pressed to defend his apostleship to the Corinthians (who were being lured by false apostles), Paul described the harsh trials he suffered for the cause of Christ. Here is a paraphrase:

> I have worked harder than those deceiving ministers. I've been imprisoned more often, whipped countless times, and faced death again and again. Five times the Jews gave me thirty-nine lashes. Three times I was beaten with rods, and once I was stoned. Three times I was shipwrecked. I spent a day and a night adrift in the deep. I journeyed many miles—in perils of waters and perils of my own countrymen, Gentiles, robbers, and false brethren. I've faced perils in the cities, in the wilderness, and in the stormy seas. I have lived with weariness, pain, and sleeplessness, and have often been hungry and thirsty and cold. And besides all that, I experience deep concern for all the churches daily (2 Cor. 11:23–28).

Jesus personally told Paul, His chosen instrument, how many things he would suffer for His name (Acts 9:16). So why did Paul become a sold-out-for-Jesus preacher when he knew in advance how much he'd suffer?

This ardent apostle tells us that he was compelled by Jesus' Calvary love for him. In response, Paul's ambition was to know and serve his Savior—who died and rose again to save priceless souls and who desired for His followers to no longer live for themselves but for Him. (See 1 Cor. 6:20; 2 Cor. 5:14–15.)

Does Christ's love for you motivate you to know Him more intimately, love Him more deeply, and serve Him more passionately? Does His divine love inspire you to give up lesser pursuits in order to spend time with Him—praying, praising, and poring over Scriptures? If so, beware: you might become a sold-out-for-Jesus evangelist yourself! And even if you don't, you'll store up treasures in heaven that you can enjoy for a long, long time.

> The love of Christ compels us…
> He died for all, that those who live should
> live no longer for themselves, but for
> Him who died for them and rose again.
> (2 Cor. 5:14–15)

RUNNING A SIX-SECOND RACE

Charlene, my fun "big sister," moved in with my family for about nine months after her dad married my mom. Char and I were teenagers at the time, and she was three years older. I enjoyed her witty humor and the delightful songs she taught me and my other two sisters. She worked long hours as a waitress and impressed me as an exquisite seamstress.

After losing contact for decades, we reconnected by e-mail. Joy flooded my heart when I learned that Char had recently become a sister in Christ. Yet my heart broke when she revealed something I never knew about, her abusive childhood.

Her parents divorced when she was one year old. Numerous nights she cried herself to sleep waiting for her mom to come back, but she never did. Her dad never hugged her or said he loved her, and he punished her with his belt. Over the years, she lived with nine foster families.

For years, my dear stepsister suffered under a cloud of depression. Even after becoming a Christian, she struggled to overcome her painful past. She felt unworthy in every area of her life—even undeserving of her Lord's love. Since I didn't know how to respond to Char's tender words, I asked for help from *Our Divine Sympathizer*, who loves her divinely and understands her pain completely.

Here are some excerpts from my reply-mail:

> Sister, you're a cherished daughter of the King and accepted in the Beloved (Eph. 1:6)! God smiles over you because you opened your heart to His Son. Although people rejected you repeatedly, you didn't turn your back on Jesus. Just think how many people have denied their Savior—even those who had good, easy lives without abuse. Yet they are heading toward eternal destruction (Matt. 7:13) and you aren't.
>
> *Our Divine Sympathizer* personally identifies with your struggles and lavishes His love on you (1 John 3:1). Whenever you express to Him what's on your heart, you will find comfort and grace (see Heb. 4:15–16). And know that God is not disappointed with you. He sees you through Jesus' righteousness—as if you're wearing a white linen robe (see 2 Cor. 5:21). As a believer, you are free from all condemnation (Rom. 8:1).
>
> Scripture tells us that our earthy life is brief. It's like a vapor that's here today and vanishes tomorrow (James 4:14). Picture a puff of mist that only lasts about six seconds. So don't lose heart. Stay focused on serving the Lord using your giftings, such as your writing and creativity, as

the Holy Spirit leads. And one day Jesus will reward you for faithful, fruitful service.

Paul the apostle likens the Christian life to an athlete running a race. We are to run with endurance to win. We do this by growing in faith and fulfilling our individual callings, while keeping our eyes on Jesus (Heb. 12:1–2). He's the author and finisher of our faith, our cheerleader along the way, and our grand prize at the end of the race. Hallelujah!

Char said she read my note of encouragement over and over—feeling refreshed, as if God were writing directly to her. In return, my sister also ministered to me. I've re-fixed my eyes on Jesus with an undivided heart.

Have you heard the Lord's voice calling you to serve Him with your spiritual giftings? If so, abide in the Vine by staying in fellowship with Jesus, and let His words abide in you (John 15:5–8). You never know how much fruit the smallest act of kindness might bring forth. And you will discover that your devotion to Him, and your delight in Him, is filling you with joy and propelling you forward in your own Christian race—all six seconds of it.

> Forgetting those things which are behind [in my past]
> and reaching forward to those things which are ahead,
> I press toward the goal [to finish my race] for the
> prize of the upward call of God in Christ Jesus.
> (Phil. 3:12–14)

A splash of living water and apologetics

CONSIDERING THE BIBLICAL WORLDVIEW

Despite hardships and afflictions in this world (which are due to humanity's fallen state and the resulting alienation from God), *Our Divine Sympathizer* gives glorious promises to His children:

1. There is purpose in our adversity (Rom. 8:28–29; 2 Cor. 4:8–18).

2. He will go through our suffering with us (Matt. 28:20; Heb. 13:5–6).

3. He will not let us be tempted beyond what we can endure (1 Cor. 10:13).

4. Someday we will experience everlasting joy in heaven, where pain and sorrow do not exist (1 Peter 1:8–9; Rev. 21:1–4).

5. We have the security of knowing that we will never be separated from His love (Rom. 8:35–39).

When we ask our compassionate Lord the age-old question *Why?*, God's answer is *Trust Me, for I have plans.*[63] And as time goes by, believers will see that pain and suffering lead to divine blessings.

***

The biblical worldview is the only one that accepts
the reality of evil and suffering while giving both the
cause and the purpose, while offering God-given
strength and sustenance in the midst of it.[64]

—Ravi Zacharias

DANCING IN THE LAND MINES

Living on the sidewalks among the homeless can be treacherous. My friend Rupert e-mailed me that he had survived ten weeks and was still waiting for a bed at St. Vincent's. From facing constant dangers and threats, he felt like he was "dancing in the land mines." Many people who slept around his campsite near the bridge were mentally ill, drug addicts, gang members, or newly released felons.

Although Rupert witnessed frequent beatings on the sidewalks, he hadn't been roped into any of them. Explainable only by God's protection, he hadn't had to use his pugilistic skills in even one altercation! However, I do suspect the fancy-footwork part of boxing came in handy when he dodged those potential explosions.

Rupert faced other challenges. For example, if the homeless were still asleep on the sidewalk by sunrise, they got cited by police officers for "illegal lodging." Most of them would go to jail for not paying the fine. Yet there was nowhere else for them to stay and no way to plug in an alarm clock (to comply with the city ordinance) even if they had one.

His job-seeking efforts led to feelings of defeat. "I'm just tossing darts into the wind," wrote Rupert, "without landing so much as one job interview from my efforts." I reminded him that although his job-search darts hadn't hit any target yet, we knew the Creator of the wind, who's able to send a gust and divinely direct a dart—sooner or later.

Despite his battle with depression, my friend trekked forward in his attempts to succeed, never abandoning his faith in God. I prayed for him with renewed hope when I saw the name of his new blog site: "Jesus Loves Rupert."

I knew God was covering and protecting him. Like the time an inebriated woman followed him around in the bridge vicinity, persistently trying to provoke him. But before she could stir up trouble, a police officer appeared and sent the woman on her way to sober up elsewhere.

Followers of Christ sometimes go through deep valleys in life without knowing why. Yet we can always trust God and His scriptural promises. He never changes, His love for us never diminishes, He will never leave us, and He works all things together for our eternal benefit.

Why not pray right now for a struggling sister or brother in Christ you know of who's facing great hardship? And perhaps give that special person a phone call? You could be a careful listener and then encourage him or her to stand on God's promises—while walking by faith through the mine fields of life.

> We walk by faith, not by sight.
> [We live by believing, not by seeing.]
> (2 Cor. 5:7)

SURRENDERING AN ALABASTER JAR

One evening, Simon hosted a dinner at his house in Bethany to honor Jesus and to celebrate Lazarus's restored life. As Jesus sat at the table, Mary (of Bethany) expressed deep love for her Lord by breaking her alabaster jar and anointing His head with the oil it contained (Matt. 26:6–13; Mark 14:3–9).[65]

Mary's extravagant act had huge significance. The estimated value of the perfumed oil was the equivalent of a person's full-time salary for one year. It was her dowry—her hope of a good marriage, future financial security, and a good reputation.

Although Judas ridiculed Mary for wasting the perfumed oil that could have been sold and the money given to the poor, Jesus gladly received her extreme act of worship. Perhaps Mary was the only disciple who understood Jesus was going to die soon (see Matt. 26:2). For Jesus told the dinner guests that Mary poured the fragrant oil on His body for His burial (v. 12). Then He said,

"Wherever this gospel is preached in the whole world, what this woman has done will also be told as a memorial to her" (v. 13).

Using the analogy of an alabaster jar, Anne Graham Lotz paints a poignant picture of our heavenly Father's extravagant love for us. Here is a condensed version:

> The most precious possession of God the Father was His beloved Son, Jesus. Yet He loved the people in the world so much that He placed His alabaster jar on a small manger bed of hay in Bethlehem. Then thirty-three years later, on a hill called Calvary (cold, and barren, and swarming with an angry mob), the Father picked up His precious alabaster jar and smashed it on a rugged, wooden cross. As the contents of flesh and blood were poured out and the fragrance of His love permeated human history forever, our tears were on His face.[66]

The Son of God demonstrated His elaborate love for us as well. *Our Divine Sympathizer*, willingly and humbly, came to earth as the priceless alabaster jar—broken and poured out for you and me, to set us free.

Thank You, Abba Father, for sacrificing Your beloved Son to redeem me. And thank You, Lord Jesus, for sacrificially dying in my place so I could live. In response to such profound love, I re-surrender my heart and life to You today. Even though others won't understand, I am willing to surrender my own alabaster jar—my most precious possession—as an extreme act of worship.

God is [pure *agapē*] love…We love
Him because He first loved us.
(1 John 4:16, 19)

WORSHIPPING GOD FOR HIS AWESOM-AZING ATTRIBUTES

He is omnibenevolent (all love/goodness), and He is omnipotent.

Dear Lord, although You're the King of the universe, You humbled Yourself and suffered for us—even personally for me. You opened Your heart up to rejection…Your body up to torture…Your soul up to agony. As my Sympathizer, You know everything about me and my struggles, and You extend empathy and favor to me. Thank You for journeying through life with me and for Your ongoing grace that flows from Your attribute of goodness. No matter what trials I face, Your love and grace are enough to get me through. In Jesus' name, amen.

THE LIGHT OF THE WORLD

Reveals Himself to Us Personally

(Jesus Christ declared:)
I am the light of the world.
He who follows Me shall not walk in
darkness, but have the light of life.
(John 8:12)

Awakened by a Brilliant Flashlight

"As Christians, we naturally thank God for the miracle of our rebirth," remarked my daughter-in-law Linda. "Yet we often forget to thank Him for our physical birth. We should be grateful for both of those wonders."

I wholeheartedly agreed with her. As I thought about her words, I pictured in my mind a mannequin in a department store, coming to life. First the statue was formed. Then it became a live person when its designer shined a brilliant flashlight on her.

After I praised God for both of the mega-wonders He did for me, I recalled the moment in my own life when God pointed a light beam at me and I was born again.

When I was in my mid-thirties and had to resign from my job after just three years, this undesired change plunged me into an identity crisis. I had worked hard to finish college and obtain my full-time paralegal position in the trial department of a large law firm. By taking night classes after work, I then obtained the ABA-approved certification for legal assistantship.

Now what was I going to do with my life?

I grew up as the daughter of a Protestant priest, and our family worshipped the God of the Bible—for which I am grateful. Yet God had always seemed distant. As a kid, I wanted a two-way relationship with Him, but I presumed He was too big and too busy to relate to my personal concerns.

My faith in God wavered during my teen years when my parents got a divorce, then fully crumbled when I took junior college courses in philosophy and comparative religions.

After my paralegal job ended, I longed to know if the God my father preached about from the pulpit was real. But in my search for purpose and fulfillment, I dipped into a mild depression.

By God's providence, I joined a women's Bible study where the worship music and Scriptures began flooding my soul. However, if I was going to surrender my whole life to God, I needed to know if Christianity was the one true religion. After all, I figured, if I had been born in China I'd probably be a Buddhist!

As I listened regularly to a Bible answer man on the radio, I discovered that there's plenty of objective evidence for the historicity of Jesus and the Bible. I also learned that Christianity isn't merely a belief system with a list of dos and don'ts, but rather a personal love relationship with the Lord. And that the Trinity is an essential Christian doctrine. My father had indeed preached about the real God!

Following a group luncheon one day, my Bible study leader told me how to be "born again" (John 3:3). That was news to me! For the first time, I understood the gospel. Jesus, the *Light of the World*, lifted my spiritual blinders so I could see (2 Cor. 4:4).

Ready to surrender my life to Him, I took a walk in my neighbor-hood park and said a simple prayer.

God, I've said a hundred prayers to You over the years, but I've never asked You to come into my heart. Please be my Lord and Savior and fill me with the Holy Spirit.

With a *whoosh*, I sensed the Lord's love flow over me, enrap-turing my heart. I awakened spiritually—like a mannequin who became a brand-new creation under God's divine spotlight. Hallelujah!

I love hearing the unique personal testimonies of fellow believers, don't you? They testify to the reality of God and the miracle that human beings can know Him personally.

If you've never written out your own story of how the Lord brought you from death to life spiritually (Eph. 2:1), why not do so now? Then ask Him who He wants you to share it with, either in person or in writing. If seekers who hear your testimony place their trust in Jesus Christ someday, more flashlights will shine life. And more people will joyfully declare, along with the psalm-ist, "The Lord is my light and my salvation" (Ps. 27:1).

> God, who is rich in mercy, because of His great
> love with which He loved us, even when we
> were dead in trespasses, made us alive together
> with Christ [He enlightened us by grace].
> (Eph. 2:4–5)

LAMPS WITH OIL
AND TRIMMED WICKS

God gave my friend Hannah a ministry using her God-given craft skills. She loves to crochet her own signature creations—including colorful baby booties, blankets, beanies, and shawls. She freely gives them to the homeless, the convalescing, and expect-ant mothers. And she enjoys tucking a gospel tract inside the items. So when the recipients get their cozy gifts, they also have the opportunity to pray and receive Jesus. If they do, they will receive the ultimate free gift—of eternal life with their Savior.

In the Sermon on the Mount, Jesus commissioned His disciples to be "the light of the world." He called us to place our lit lamps on a lampstand for others to see. Like a city high on a hill, glowing in the night, we are to display our good works and our love for one another (Matt. 5:14–16).

The lamps used in Jesus' day required oil and trimmed wicks. Oil was the active agent, and wicks needed to be snipped so they wouldn't produce smoke. Likewise, we need our lamps replenished with oil by refilling our hearts with the Holy Spirit—through prayer, worship, and Scripture meditation. We can keep our wicks trimmed by examining ourselves and bringing our lives into conformity with God's Word.[67] My friend Hannah does this by praying in the mornings for God to refill her with the Holy Spirit and to work into her life the "fruit of the Spirit" (Gal. 5:22–23).

If you keep your heart filled with the Holy Spirit and your life in alignment with the Word of God, the light of our awesom-azing God will shine in and through you. And if you serve Him using the spiritual gifts He has given you, God will set more hearts aglow with His love. Priceless souls will be drawn closer to Jesus. And some of them might choose to live in the light of His glorious presence.

What a marvelous array of lights His redeemed people will behold someday in heaven!

- We will see flashes of lightning (Rev. 4:5; 11:19).

- We will see the radiant, green-hued rainbow that surrounds God's throne (Rev. 4:3).

- We will see the One whose countenance shines like the brilliant sun (Rev. 1:16).

- We will dwell with the One who said, "Let there be light," and there was light (Gen. 1:3).

I know Hannah will be there. And perhaps people wearing crocheted beanies and booties, who saw the light of Christ through her gracious gifts. But one thing is for sure. All people who have become spiritually reborn are God's signature creations.

> Let your light so shine before men,
> that they may see your good works and
> glorify your Father in heaven.
> (Matt. 5:16)

A BEGGAR BECOMES A BOASTER

Twice in Scripture Jesus declared, "I am the light of the world" (John 8:12; 9:5). By this extreme declaration, He equated Himself to the great I AM—Jehovah, the eternal God who appeared to Moses at the burning bush in Exodus 3:2.

In John chapter 9, we read that Jesus gave sight to a blind beggar. After anointing the man's eyes with mud, Jesus instructed him to go wash in the Pool of Siloam. He did so immediately and received the gift of vision.

When questioned by the Pharisees, the healed man boldly said, "Since the world began, it has been unheard of that anyone opened the eyes of one who was born blind. If this Man were not from God, He could do nothing" (vv. 32–33). And the Pharisees cast him out of their presence. The beggar had become a boaster of Jesus Christ even though he hadn't visibly seen Him yet.

Jesus then found the man and asked him, "Do you believe in the Son of God?"

"Who is He, Lord, that I may believe in Him?" the man replied.

"You have both seen Him and it is He who is talking with you."

"Lord, I believe!" the man professed. Then he worshipped the *Light of the World* standing in his very presence (vv. 35–38).

As preordained, God's miraculous works were revealed in the blind man's life. He had lived in complete darkness since birth, yet Jesus opened his eyes to see the light both physically and spiritually. Even today, that man's testimony is bringing forth spiritual fruit for the kingdom.

Jesus compassionately healed each of us too. As regenerated men and women, we can now pass on the message that at the cross, Jesus turned on the light of salvation and brought beauty out of the ashes of humanity. If we do, the wondrous works of God will be shown in our lives as they were in the blind man's life. We too will be blind people who received sight and beggars who became boasters.

> The true Light [Jesus] gives light to every man
> who comes into the world [providing the
> opportunity for anyone to join God's family].
> (John 1:9)

A splash of apologetics concerning God's revelatory light

IS THE BIBLE INFALLIBLE?

There is compelling evidence for the Bible's infallibility, based on the three tests of historiography and literary criticism used to investigate historical documents (the internal test, the external test, and the bibliographical test).[68] Some of the evidence is highlighted below:

- Hundreds of undisputed archaeological discoveries that confirm the Bible's historical references. (No archaeological discoveries have disputed the Bible's text.)

- The accurate fulfillment of three hundred Old Testament messianic prophecies by Jesus of Nazareth in the first century (sixty-one of which are major messianic prophecies).

- The amazing unity and harmony of all sixty-six books comprising the Bible, written by forty different authors over 1,500 years and in three different languages on three continents.

- Extensive manuscript evidence for the New Testament's integrity, based on comparisons of thousands of New Testament manuscripts, as well as confirmation by the writings of the early church fathers (which quote nearly the whole New Testament).

- Extensive manuscript evidence for the Old Testament's integrity, based on comparisons with the Greek Septuagint and with Old Testament texts from Palestine, Syria, and Egypt, as well as confirmation by the uncovered Dead Sea Scrolls.

(For an overview of the evidence for the Bible's infallibility, see the endnote.[69])

THE LIGHT OF SCRIPTURE

When I discovered that my close friend Miranda was battling lung cancer in an advanced stage, my emotions flipped back and forth between peace and panic. She was a lovely redhead, a married woman with two sons, an accomplished pianist and ballet dancer, but not yet born again.

Miranda's two other best friends were a Mormon and a New Ager. Each of us visited Miranda at her home regularly as she proceeded through chemo treatments and home care. Since I desperately wanted to know how best to minister to her, I drove to a prayer meeting at my church. The intercessors prayed for my friend, and they counseled me to ask God to protect her from false notions and bring the truth of the gospel into her heart.

One night, while reading my Bible, a Scripture stood off the page like a flash of light. The context was Jesus instructing His disciples to spread the gospel, despite opposition, while depending on the Holy Spirit (Mark 13:11). I turned off my lamp and went to sleep, treasuring the Lord's word of assurance to me. I knew that the next day He'd reveal to me just what to say to my friend.

The following morning I drove Miranda to Cedars-Sinai Hospital for her chemotherapy. As we sat in the lobby waiting for her name to be called, she surprised me by asking, "Marilyn, do you think I'll go to heaven when I die?"

"I don't know," I replied with compassion, "but I do know how you can be sure." I took out of my wallet a small gospel tract called "Steps to Peace with God"[70] and read it out loud. Miranda looked on with great interest. The pamphlet ended with a suggested prayer of salvation. When I asked my dear friend if she wanted to pray it, she reached over and lifted the tract out of my hand, then recited the prayer to receive Christ. The light of God's Word seemed to flood the lobby and light up Miranda's face.

For many more months, Miranda enjoyed quality life and blessed others' lives as well. Now I suspect she is dancing—in a divine spotlight—with the *Light of the World* Himself.

God's children will someday enjoy complete fellowship with the Lord face-to-face, no longer seeing Him dimly as through a mirror (1 Cor. 13:12). Are you living in anticipation of that privilege? If not, maybe it's time for a personal revival. Why not consider returning to the cross and rededicating yourself to live for Jesus now. After all, our earthly lives are only a blip on the radar screen of eternity (James 4:14).

> When [Jesus] is revealed, we shall be like
> Him [complete in Christ], for we shall
> see Him as He is [clearly, in a new light].
> (1 John 3:2)

SCRIPTURES BURNING IN OUR HEARTS

Just hours after the resurrected Jesus walked out of His tomb, He joined two of His disciples walking to the village of Emmaus (Luke 24:13–35). Neither disciple recognized Him. But as the three of them traveled and conversed, Jesus illuminated the meaning of Scriptures and their hearts burned within them.

Beginning with Moses and all the prophets, He revealed how the messianic prophecies pertained to Him (v. 27). For example, He told them that the Savior would come to rescue people's souls, that suffering was His path to glory, and that someday He'd return as the conquering King.

Toward evening, when they reached the village, the two disciples asked Jesus to remain awhile, and He lingered. As they began to dine together, He blessed and broke bread. At that point the disciples recognized Jesus—perhaps from seeing His scarred hands holding the bread. When their eyes opened, He vanished from their sight. That very hour, they returned to Jerusalem and reported their encounter with the risen Lord (vv. 28–35).

The *Light of the World* loves to meet with us, His present-day disciples, when we open our Bibles and hearts to know more of Him, His truth, and His love (Eph. 1:16–18). And if we ask Him to linger a while, His answer will always be yes.

One Bible commentator explains how Scripture can burn in our hearts and affect our lives the way it did with Cleopas and his fellow traveler:

> As Jesus spoke to them from the Scriptures, the fire in their hearts was fanned into a flame, and they knew it was true [that the Lord had risen]. They couldn't wait to go out and tell the others. If the fire burns low in our lives, how we need to sit at Jesus' feet and hear from His Word! Then, as our hearts begin to burn once again, as we get on fire for Him, we will go out to share the good news.[71]

When we gather in Jesus' name with other believers, He promises to be right there in our midst (Matt. 18:19–20). When I walk with my prayer partner Nancy along the city's water channel, sometimes I sense that the Messiah is walking there with us—inspiring our prayers and expounding the meaning of His Word to us.

As you journey with Jesus along the road of life, seek Him at every turn. When you listen for His voice as you read the Bible, the Holy Spirit will reveal to you the deep things of God through the light of Scripture (1 Cor. 2:10, 13). And as He teaches you spiritual truths about the Messiah, don't be surprised if the fire in your heart "fans into a flame."

(The two disciples said:)
Did not our heart burn within us while He talked
with us on the road, and while He opened
[illuminated] the Scriptures to us?
(Luke 24:32)

Capturing splashes of living water

KEEPING A JESUS JOURNAL

One thrilling way to deepen your intimacy with Jesus, the *Light of the World*, is to keep a personal journal of your walk with Him. You will become more enamored with Him than ever, and your faith in Him will steadily increase.

In a notebook or online, you can record your experiences with our awesom-azing God (see John 15:4–11). You might, for example, describe scriptural insights He gives you. Or write out prayers, praises, and answers to prayer. To give it a scrapbook flavor, you could paste special notes, graphics, or photos inside.

Your writings will reveal how God shines His light into your life—leading, teaching, anointing, protecting, and blessing. These recollections will encourage you to see (and expect) God's hand in your life every day.

Another benefit of journaling is that it will remind you to "log in" time with Jesus regularly. It will also keep the Enemy from sowing doubts or fears in your heart when you face challenges because you've focused on Jesus' faithfulness.

In the future, your journals can be a testimony to your children, and others, of God's miraculous works in your life as you stack up "stones of remembrance" (see Joshua 4).

Sharing God's Word with a Hare Krishna

My friend Joanie and I reached out to a Hare Krishna who sold toys at a kiosk in the shopping mall. He referred to himself by the name of a Hindu god, but he let us call him Jason. After friendly greetings, we asked if he knew about Jesus in the Bible. He said he had grown up in the Catholic church and used to believe in the Trinity. But some "saintly" Hare Krishnas had attracted him to their faith, and now he was in the process of "overcoming bad karma with good karma."

For thirty minutes or so, Joanie and I sat on a stone planter and listened to Jason talk. (Fortunately, no customers came by.) It grieved my heart to know he was under the grip of a false religion that would separate him from Christ forever. I silently prayed that the Lord would anoint our words and that Jason would hear in his heart the voice of the Good Shepherd calling him back into the light.

I pointed out to Jason that the Bible teaches Jesus Christ is supreme over all gods and all religious systems. Then I asked if he had ever read the book of John. He couldn't recall. Since I had just studied John in a women's Bible study, I recited the two opening verses of chapter 1. As I spoke, I sensed the Holy Spirit's empowering. Jason must have sensed it too, because he stepped back like he was amazed and exclaimed, "Whoa!"

When customers began to appear, Joanie and I gave him an apologetics pamphlet on the Trinity,[72] then left his booth. Later we prayed that the Holy Spirit would speak to Jason through the Scriptures in the tract.

Sowing the seeds of God's truth is a venture in faith (see John 4:35–38). We may not realize fruit from our efforts for a long time (maybe not until we see the saints go marchin' in!). But I do know this: if you ask the Lord to set up divine appointments for you to witness of Him to beloved unbelievers, He will do so and He will be there to guide you (see Matt. 28:18–20).

During such conversations, there's a good chance the Holy Spirit will bring to your remembrance a specific Scripture to share—as He did for me with Jason—that will speak truth and enlightenment to a soul lost in darkness and deceit. For the *Light of the World* came to set the captives free. And God's Word never returns to Him void or empty, but accomplishes what He pleases (Isa. 55:11).

> In the beginning was the Word [Christ, the *Logos*],
> and the Word was with God, and the Word
> was God. He was in the beginning with God.
> (John 1:1–2)

CHRISTIANITY, THE MOST HUMBLE FAITH

After my encounter with Jason, I continued to grieve for his spiritual condition. So I typed a caring note to him. It contained scriptural truth and light, evidence concerning who Jesus is, and my concern for his salvation.

First I addressed Jason's comment about the "saintly" Hare Krishnas who had attracted him to their faith. I suspect he meant that they showed less pride than people he had met in other religions. However, biblical Christianity is the humblest faith ever. For the Bible emphasizes there is absolutely nothing we could do ourselves to earn salvation (Eph. 2:8–9) or to add to the finished work of Jesus on the cross (Rom. 4:4; Gal. 2:21).

My note to Jason explained it this way:

> In the overall cosmic conflict, Jesus Christ defeated Satan on our behalf. When Jesus purchased our salvation on the cross, He declared, "It is finished!" (John 19:30). That's grace. That's divine love. That's staggering. All we can do is hold out our hands and receive God's free gift. That profound truth is humbling indeed. *Hallelujah!*

I also addressed his comment about overcoming bad karma with good karma:

> At Calvary, Jesus in effect worked off all the "bad karma" for us, once and for all. It's a done deal! The sinless One, the perfect Lamb of God, took away the sins of the world by taking our punishment on His own shoulders. As a result, God the Father views believers through Christ's righteousness—as perfected saints heading for heaven to live with Him (2 Cor. 5:21). We can receive this miracle by saying a heartfelt prayer asking Jesus to be our Lord and Savior. As soon as we do, we are eternally forgiven for all our sins. (Yet it does take time to process these spiritual riches in our minds!)

After praying over the note, I drove to the mall to give it to Jason. He wasn't at the kiosk, but two other Hare Krishnas were there. They promised to deliver my envelope to Jason and asked if they could read the contents first. I smiled and gladly gave them permission. Then I headed for the escalator, marveling over their question.

I would love to see Jason and his friends in heaven someday, worshiping the true and living God. Kindly pray for them—and for any other Hare Krishnas you may know of—that they will come to the realization that Jesus Christ is supreme. For there is a name that is above every other name (Phil. 2:9–11). There is one Savior whom lost souls can call upon to be assured of stepping into heaven's everlasting light (Acts 4:12).

> (God the Father said to His Son:)
> I will also give You as a light to the Gentiles,
> that You should be My salvation to the ends of the earth.
> (Isa. 49:6)

"I'VE BEEN PRAYING MY FACE OFF!"

In another e-mail, Rupert told me he was "praying his face off" for a breakthrough in his circumstances. For three months, he was stuck on the sidewalks with no income. The hardships he endured during that time are difficult for me to imagine.

For an early birthday gift, my husband and I gave Rupert spending money and an Amtrak ticket to be our weekend guest. That Sunday, we all worshipped at a local church pastored by a former mentor of Rupert's. The preacher's message really spoke to him, he told me later. The light of God's Word reminded my friend that God had a plan for his life.

After lunch, Rupert decided to look for a used bicycle at a thrift shop, and I tagged along. The only bike we could find that afternoon had two flat tires, which prevented him from test-riding it, but Rupert bought it anyway. At a nearby bike shop he purchased two inner tubes and a lock, then pumped up the tires.

We hustled to the Amtrak station. A smile lit up Rupert's face as he sat on his new bike, waiting for the train. When it came, he loaded his bike on the back and hopped aboard to return to San Diego. The next day I received this e-mail:

The good news is that this bike is unusually balanced and lightweight, so it is very fast for a hybrid model. "Specialized" makes top-quality bikes, but I had never heard of their hybrids. So I had no idea what to expect. The quality is very high. My average speed is around 20 miles an hour. It is all flat around here, so I'm flying! The brakes stop me on a dime. So between me and the cars, it is a high-speed ballet that reminds me how much fun pedaling can be. I would give this bike an appraisal value of around $200. Factoring in the performance element, it is top shelf! Thank you once again for this blessing.

Rupert's persistent, praying-his-face-off petitions must have lined up with God's will (1 John 5:14–15). I believe God will also bring him a breakthrough in other circumstances, airlifting him off the sidewalks soon. In the meantime, at least he will have an enjoyable form of transportation—sort of a rapid transit with his high-speed *bicycle ballet.*

Hearing that God has a plan for our lives can renew our sense of purpose (Eph. 2:10). I pray that my friend will refresh his relationship with Jesus by daily staying in prayer and in the Scripture. That's the only way we can consistently live for Christ.

Do you meditate on God's Word each day? If so, you are accessing infinite wisdom from the Lover of your soul. And you will stay on track with God's plan, following the light of truth.

> Your word is a lamp to my feet
> and a light [like a flashlight] to my path.
> (Psalm 119:105)

Splashes of living water and apologetics

THE BIBLE'S UNIQUENESS

The Bible is unparalleled by any other book that is regarded as sacred literature. Consider its unity, continuity, circulation, translation, survival, and teachings (which include numerous predictive prophecies, centuries of ancient history, and the frank portrayal of its characters' sins and faults).

The Bible is distinct in its influence on literature; e.g., by its inspiration on countless literary writers. It is also distinct in its effect on civilization; e.g., by its unexcelled depth of morality in the principles of Christian love.[73]

The Bible itself claims to be God's revelation to mankind. It teaches that Scripture is: authoritative (John 17:17), living (Heb. 4:12), perfect (Ps. 19:7), sharp (Heb. 4:12), pure (Prov. 30:5), powerful (Heb. 4:12), infallible (Matt. 5:18), nourishing (Deut. 8:3), light (Ps. 119:105), truth (Ps. 119:160), and final and complete (Jude 3).

* * *

For You have magnified Your word
above all Your name.
(Ps. 138:2)

WALKING AS CHILDREN OF THE LIGHT

One morning, after walking along the sidewalk trail that loops around my condominium complex, I sat on a park bench beside a pine tree to read my Bible and meet with the Lord. Moments later a gardener's truck stalled right in front of me, emitting smoke and noxious fumes. I chuckled, identifying a probable ploy by the Enemy to sabotage my devotional time. I closed my Bible and decided to wait for the smog to lift.

But in trying to restart his vehicle, the gardener ground his gears over and over again. The screeching noise made it impossible for me to focus on the Lord—even after stuffing my ears with tissue. Finally I sprinted away from my bench, with plugged nose and plugged ears, in search of a more conducive location.

After trying other outdoor settings without success, I returned home and settled down at my dining room table with my Bible, journal, and pen. Although my valued quiet time had been cut shorter, at least the Enemy didn't thwart my plans altogether.

That scenario is indicative of the Christian's spiritual battle. Our Adversary tries to stop us from wearing our mighty-in-God armor, especially by interrupting our times in the Bible and prayer—our two offensive weapons (see Eph. 6:10–18). He wants to keep us from communion with the Lover of our souls and from growing in God's Word. For when we do those things, we discover God's will for our lives and realize how perfect His will really is (see Rom. 12:2).

Believers are spiritually wealthy beyond belief. Accordingly, we are called to "walk as children of light" (Eph. 5:8) and reflect God's goodness. To walk in the light consistently, we need to be filled by the Holy Spirit repeatedly—which comes through confessing our sins and yielding to God.[74]

By walking as children of light empowered by God's Spirit, we are able to do such things as: love others as Christ loved us (sacrificially); reveal goodness, righteousness, and truth; take no part in deeds of darkness; walk cautiously and wisely; seize opportunities to bring glory to God; and understand God's will by knowing His Word (Eph. 5:1–17).

The three signs of the Spirit-filled life are being joyful, thankful, and submissive (vv. 18–21). Do you find yourself making music to the Lord in your heart, giving Him thanks for all things, and humbly submitting to others out of your devotion to Him? If so, you are living a Spirit-filled life.

If not, spend time with the Lord each day in prayer and Bible reading (even if you need to tote along tissues, nose plugs, and sprinting shoes!) As a result, you will yield to God's will more and more. Then you will be refilled with the Spirit repeatedly… equipped to prevail in spiritual warfare…and prepared to walk as a child of the light.

> For you were once darkness [your hearts
> were full of darkness], but now
> you are light in the Lord.
> [Therefore] walk as children of light.
> (Eph. 5:8)

INTO HIS MARVELOUS LIGHT

"The Light broke through and I could see it all so clearly," writes Carol Wild in *Redeemed and Restored*. "I knew I was a sinner in need of a Savior."[75] In this compilation of pastors' wives' testimonies, she relates her experience when she and her husband, Malcolm, became spiritually reborn (John 3:3).

That night Carol understood the life-changing truth that Jesus Christ died on the cross for her personally—not only collectively for the sins of all humanity. The two spouses knelt on the floor of a pastor's office in England and asked the Lord to forgive them and come into their lives.

> Wow, did I feel clean! As we drove home I told Malcolm that if I died right then, I knew I would be going to heaven…I had given my life to Jesus, and therefore my name was written in the Lamb's Book of Life. I imagined the Lord with a pen in His hand writing my name in this big book. I pictured red ink flowing from the pen as He wrote, and the ink was His blood (Rev. 3:5; 21:27).

Isaiah 9:2 says, "The people who walked in darkness have seen a great light; those who dwelt in the land of the shadow of death, upon them a light has shined." This is what happened to me: Once I walked in darkness, but now I have seen the Light—I have seen Jesus![76]

Today Malcolm and Carol pastor a church in Florida. During their thirty-plus years in ministry, they have no doubt shared Jesus with many other people whose names are now written in the Lamb's Book of Life. They too follow the *Light of the World* instead of the god of this world—no longer walking in darkness but walking in light (John 8:12).

Are you marveling right now over Jesus' title as *Light of the World?* He is pure spiritual light in His essence, and He is the source of all spiritual illumination (John 8:32; 1 John 1:5).[77]

Light will expose and drive out darkness. Light will bring life. Light will shine forth God's glory. And Light will open unbelievers' spiritual eyes. So let's be ready reflectors of His light. After all, the Lamb's Book of Life keeps expanding every day.

[God's] own special people…proclaim
the praises of Him who called [them]
out of darkness into His marvelous light.
(1 Pet. 2:9)

WORSHIPPING GOD FOR HIS AWESOM-AZING ATTRIBUTES

He is light, He is beauty, and He is transcendent.

Lord God, I worship You as the Light of the World, who has called me out of the darkness into Your marvelous light so I could live with You. Thank You for shining Your astonishing love on me and for giving me spiritual illumination as I read Your Word. I stand in awe of You, the Radiant One whose beauty and goodness are reflected in crea-

tion. I am so grateful that even though You transcend time and space, You are part of my personal life.[78] *I remain ever devoted to You, my light and my salvation. In Jesus' name, amen.*

OUR ROYAL REDEEMER

RESCUES US AND
BRINGS US VICTORIES

*I [Paul] declare to you the gospel…that Christ
died for our sins according to the Scriptures,
and that He was buried, and that He rose again
the third day according to the Scriptures.
(1 Cor. 15:1–4)*

THE OLIVE GROVE AT GETHSEMANE

NOT MANY EARS heard my dad deliver a poignant sermon during Passion Week decades ago, standing behind a plywood pulpit in our small traditional church. I too missed his message about Jesus in the garden of Gethsemane, since my twin sister and I were probably sitting in Sunday school, coloring pictures of Jesus kneeling in prayer.

The transcript of dad's homily, the only one ever magazine-published, is now archived somewhere in Rochester, New York. Although I've been unable to track it down and read it, it thrills my heart to know that Dad waded through deep scriptural waters to hear the heartbeat of *Our Royal Redeemer* just hours before He submitted to the cross. Thinking about Dad's preaching on that topic inspired me to write this devotional piece.

Can you imagine the intensity of Jesus's prayers in the Garden of Olives on the night before His crucifixion? The word Gethsemane ("oil press place") was fitting because Jesus was crushed by the horrors of the cross awaiting Him—so much so that His sweat became like great drops of blood (Luke 22:44). He knew God's eternal plan for the sinless Lamb of God to redeem mankind. Soon, all of our iniquities would be poured into Him as our sin offering. Soon, He'd face thorns, stakes, pain, and shame. And soon, the Father's wrath would fall upon His shoulders, breaking their loving fellowship.

Yet even though Jesus' soul was "exceedingly sorrowful, even to death" (Matt. 26:38), He displayed His love and obedience to the Father—and His love for you and me—by submitting to be led to the slaughter. Three times in the olive garden that night, the Lamb of God prayed to the Father to remove the cup if possible, yet ended with these words of surrender—"Nevertheless, not as I will, but as You will" (v. 39).

All the spiritual hosts in heavenly places wrestled and rallied over the cosmos-splitting event at hand. Did the disciples understand that Gethsemane was Jesus' last stop before His betrayal, arrest, and crucifixion? Jesus asked them to stay alert and watch with Him while He prayed for strength. He explained to them (and to us) a powerful principle concerning temptation: that when our bodies are weak, even though our spirits are willing, we must pray that temptation will not overpower us (Mark 14:38). Yet instead of watching with Jesus even one hour, or praying or encouraging Him, the disciples fell asleep three times.

The stage was set, and the curtain would soon fall. *Our Royal Redeemer* was destined to fulfill the plan of God prearranged before time began. Jesus would be taken by lawless hands, nailed to a cross, and put to death (Acts 2:23–24).[79]

I'm sure my dad's message helped parishioners and magazine readers to sense the gravity of Gethsemane and Jesus' purposeful prayers. Yet even if all the pastors in the world were silent, and all the Bibles were destroyed, creation would still glorify Him endlessly. For the mighty message of *Our Royal Redeemer* and His victory on the cross is permanently archived in the heavenlies.

Is Jesus' glorious victory at Calvary etched in your heart as well? If not, ask God to let the significance of His crucifixion impact your life more deeply. If you do, surely you will worship and serve Him more fervently. You will appreciate more fully our Savior's submission to the Father in the olive garden. And you will more readily surrender your own will to our heavenly Father's will—in response to His unexplainable love.

> [Jesus] fell on His face, and prayed, saying, "O My Father, if it is possible, let this cup pass from Me; nevertheless, not as I will, but as You will."
> (Matt. 26:39)

A poem splashing living water

JUST HOURS AWAY

Just hours away
on the very next day,
> the Lamb of God, regarded as slain before the foundation of the world, would be nailed to a cross (Rev. 13:8).

Just hours away
on the very next day,
> the sinless Son would become our sin offering, allowing the wrath of God to fall upon His own shoulders (2 Cor. 5:21).

Just hours away
on the very next day,
> the Lord of glory would be crucified in order to defeat the devil and his power of death (Heb. 2:14).

> Just hours away
> *on the very next day,*
>   the almighty God would become the ultimate Servant
>   to demonstrate His deep, sacrificial love for us (John
>   15:13).
>
> Yet in the fullness of time
> *on another day,*
>   our Royal Redeemer will take back the title deed to
>   earth and open up heaven's door for us (Rev. 5:1–7).

PEDALING LIKE A JUNE BUG

After ninety-eight brutal days of camping on the sidewalks, my friend Rupert finally received a bed assignment in the men's dormitory at St. Vincent's. God's providential hand sustained him through his *Hellapalooza* season. What a relief!

His intake evaluation disclosed that he suffered from clinical depression, undiagnosed for many years. That explains why more than once he told me he felt trapped in a "hurt locker." Now, finally, my friend would be treated for that condition through the VA hospital at no charge.

Another consolation to me was that Rupert's thrift-store bicycle continued to provide him with transportation and recreation. In fact, he became quite the urban bike rider. Check out this lively testimony he shared with me—a "pedal drama" that I shortened from one of his e-mails:

> My pedaling has become outrageous. I try to point myself toward safer routes in San Diego traffic, but as pedestrians and objects populate, I'm darting and weaving like an out-of-control June bug.

Yesterday I raced a young guy down Imperial Boulevard. His boasting was getting to me, and when we neared "his block," I knew I was in a spot. I was twice as old as him, my bike was twenty years older than his, and this was not a road I traveled on much, so I didn't know it well. It was bumpy and uneven.

There was a good-sized crowd to witness my impending loss, and I thought I'd made a *big* mistake. Then I remembered…I enjoy riding, and I do it often, and I ride a lot of hills. So essentially, I train every day. I had all the tools I needed. And my bike was swift and amazingly steady. I said a panic-filled prayer, feeling like I was heading for a gunfight with Doc Holliday.

We rode up the block about a quarter mile. We stopped at a red light in the right lane, in front of cars. When the light turned green, I was primed to make a great start, but my foot slipped off the pedal.

The kid took off and got about two bike lengths ahead of me. Then I started to lean in and draft. In the blink of an eye, I felt God's hand on my bike. I really could! It was like having an invisible edge. I kept gaining on him, until I was within a tire away.

When I saw the light at the trolley tracks, designated as the finish line, I made my push. I got into a strong cadence when I had about 150 yards to go. I felt he was at his maximum speed, and he was losing his stamina. I could smell blood in the water like a shark.

I cruised right by him at about 32 miles an hour, gaining speed as I flew past the light. I beat him by a bike length and a half. It was awesome. I know God had His hand in that win. Yeah, I put my work in, but God dominated! To answer your question, Marilyn, my faith is not gone.

I'm so thankful my friend is a believer in Jesus Christ—the One who endured the ultimate "hurt locker" on the cross to secure our salvation. Then He rose from the dead, proving to be the sinless Son of God. As Rupert once said, "I don't know of anybody else who got up three days after he died and then walked away. Do you?"

Now, that's a powerful apologetic!

> [Paul] reasoned with them from the Scriptures,
> explaining and demonstrating that the Christ had to
> suffer and rise again from the dead, and saying,
> "This Jesus whom I preach to you is the Christ."
> (Acts 17:2–3)

SHARING THE RADICALLY RISEN SAVIOR

When my sister-in-Christ Joanie and I go shopping together, we pray in advance and then look for opportunities to share Jesus as we chat with people (see 1 Cor. 9:22–23). One night at the mall, we befriended a Persian fellow (a generation younger than us) selling jewelry in the mall corridor. Farid, who spoke both English and Farsi, was a genial guy and a former Muslim. He told us he believed all religions are fine.

"So you believe that all roads lead to God?" Joanie asked.

Farid said yes, then expressed some interest in the biblical Jesus. He told us he had attended a Bible study for one year. I felt relieved that at least he was convinced Islam was not the true religion. He even explained some of its teachings he disagreed with.

I asked Farid if I could share a hypothetical situation with him, and he nodded.

"What if someone died and went to the undiscovered territory, then came back to earth to tell us about it?"

"Then I would listen to him," he replied with a big smile.

"Well, that's what Jesus did! After He died, He went to the uncharted land. But on the third day, He rose from the dead and returned to earth. Then, for the next forty days, He taught people about the kingdom of God and performed many miracles. That's how we know Jesus is alive today!"

Farid seemed to ponder that.

Joanie told him how much the risen Savior loved him. Then she asked me if I had a pamphlet to give him. I pulled out of my luggage-sized purse an apologetics tract that presented evidence for the resurrection, and I offered it to him.[80]

As a customer approached the jewelry booth, Farid took my tract and said he'd read it. My friend and I waved good-bye and left. We prayed that the Holy Spirit would draw Farid to read the tract and hear the Lord's voice through the Scriptures printed inside—such as the verse where Jesus declares He is "the resurrection and the life" (John 11:25).

Only *Our Royal Redeemer* can make that claim with validity. He alone fits the credentials of the long-awaited Savior. He alone conquered death. (See Isa. 53:4–5.)

Thank You, Lord Jesus, for accomplishing that miraculous feat. Because You rose from the dead, believers will never die. Instead, we will someday transition from our earthly life to our eternal (heavenly) life. That's a profound truth—realized by everyone who receives our radically risen Savior.

(Jesus Christ said:)
I am the resurrection, and the life. He who
believes in Me, though he may die, he shall live.
(John 11:25)

A Supernatural Sign for Farid

The next time my friend Joanie and I met up with Farid at the mall, he told us that in order for him to believe in the Jesus of the Bible, he needed a sign from God.

Joanie asked, "What would such a sign look like?"

"I don't know."

She grinned. "Then how would you recognize a sign if one came to you?"

We all three chuckled. Our Persian friend rolled his eyes as if to say, *Come on, now, you two!* We promised him we'd pray for God to send a supernatural sign to him.

After the mall closed that night, my witnessing partner and I stood in the parking lot, praying for the Lord to water the seeds of truth we had planted while shopping. Just then Farid dashed toward us, saying, "Excuse me, but you're standing behind my car, and I need to back out and go home."

As we stepped aside, Joanie called out, "Farid, that's your sign! Of all the hundreds of cars parked out here, we happened to be standing and praying right behind *yours*."

He scrambled into the driver's seat and joked back to us, "Well, that might be *your* sign, but it's not mine."

Over the next few years, every time Joanie and I saw Farid at his kiosk, we asked if he had received a sign yet. But he hadn't.

Once, I ran into the mall for a quick errand and happened to pass his booth. Leaning over his laptop, he told me he was reading birthday wishes online from his friends. I smiled and kept walking, then phoned Joanie with an idea she liked. Down the hall I purchased a birthday card for Farid and signed our names to it. Inside, I tucked a gospel tract presenting the way to salvation, titled "The Best Gift in the World,"[81] and delivered it to him.

I prayed that Farid would consider the tract as his sign from God. How great it would be, I thought, if he'd take the message to heart and get spiritually reborn on the day of his physical birth. Then he could start a relationship with Jesus—the best Gift he could ever receive!

Do you carry a gospel tract in your wallet, backpack, or laptop case? When an opportunity presents itself, you might wish you had one at your fingertips. Just think, if you pass on the good news to someone who's ready to hear, he or she might respond to the Holy Spirit…recognize the ultimate heaven-sent sign… and enjoy celebrating birthdays forever with *Our Royal Redeemer*.

Thanks be to God for His indescribable gift
[Jesus Christ, the author of our salvation,
who is too wonderful for words]!
(2 Cor. 9:15)

A splash of apologetics to share

HISTORICITY OF JESUS' RESURRECTION

The four gospel accounts harmonize completely, yet each one presents a distinct focus. The apostle Matthew emphasizes Jesus as the Messiah-King, Mark emphasizes Jesus as the Suffering Servant, Luke emphasizes Jesus as the perfect Son of Man, and John emphasizes Jesus in His deity as the Son of God.[82]

The fact that we have four descriptions from various angles, all of which harmonize and amplify one another, presents a powerful apologetic for the reliability of the Bible. For it precludes any collusion.[83]

All four accounts, for example, attest to the historicity of Jesus' resurrection. The major message of all of them is: Christ died on the cross, rose from the dead, and rescues our souls so we may live. The promised Messiah carried out God's redemptive plan.

(See endnote for the classic book by Simon Greenleaf, which harmonizes the gospel accounts based on the legal rules of evidence.[84])

THE SIGN OF JONAH

The religious leaders asked Jesus for a miraculous sign to validate His ministry and claims (Matt. 12:38–41). He responded by giving them only one sign: "For as Jonah was three days and three nights in the belly of the great fish, so will the Son of Man be three days and three nights in the heart of the earth" (v. 40).[85]

Jonah's experience foreshadowed Jesus' resurrection from the dead. When comparing the two events, we see some surprising similarities and contrasts:

- *Both men were imprisoned three days and nights in the grave, yet survived.*

  Jonah returned from the belly of the fish.

  Jesus returned from the heart of the earth.

- *Both preached messages that led people to repent.*

  Jonah preached judgment and doom to the Ninevites.

  Jesus preached forgiveness and salvation for all humanity.

- *Both returned to life marred physically from enduring torture.*

  Jonah became damaged by digestive juices inside the belly of the great fish.

  Jesus became disfigured beyond human recognition on the cross.

- *Both sacrificed their lives to satisfy God's wrath coming upon others.*

  Jonah was ransomed for sailors lost at sea.

  Jesus was ransomed for the sins of many.[86]

Of course, no human effort could ever come close to the miracle of the resurrection of Jesus Christ. It demonstrated that the long-predicted Messiah had come and that His work on the cross was complete.[87] The entire Godhead was involved in the resurrection: *God the Father* powerfully raised *Jesus Christ* from the dead by means of the *Holy Spirit*. (See John 10:17; Acts 4:10; Rom. 1:4; 8:11.)

Our Royal Redeemer cried out, "It is finished!" after He shed His precious blood on the cross, conquering sin and death. Those three simple yet impactful words convey our Creator's deep love for us. Shall we post a banner of love over our hearts in deep devotion to Him? After all, His unfailing love has carried us from eternal punishment to eternal rewards. And His banner over us is love (Song 2:4).

> God demonstrates His own love toward us,
> in that while we were still sinners
> [utterly helpless], Christ died for us.
> (Rom. 5:8)

GETTING DRENCHED IN THE WORD OF GOD

At Easter time one year, I decided to soak up some of the Scriptures pertaining to Resurrection Sunday. I prayed for God to drench me in His Word so I could hear from Him and relate to the disciples' joyful discovery that their recently crucified leader became *Our Royal Redeemer*.

As I pictured the women at the tomb and pondered their visits, I came up with a few questions regarding the sequence of events.[88] Was Mary Magdalene the only woman to arrive "while it was still dark" (John 20:1)? After Mary informed Peter and John of the empty tomb, did she bring "the other Mary" back to the tomb with her (Matt. 28:1)? And when did she join the other women of Galilee who arrived at dawn with spices to anoint Jesus' body—and who told the apostles about Jesus' resurrection (Luke 24:1, 10)?

I guess I won't find out these *timing* details until I talk to Mary Magdalene myself, but one thing is clear: the angels instructed the women that morning to proclaim to the disciples that Jesus had risen from the dead and then to go meet Him in Galilee (Matt. 28:7). I can't imagine any greater news than that, can you? As for those disciples who accepted the news, joy must have filled the air and flooded their hearts.

I flipped the pages of my Bible, ready to drench myself again. I wanted to read about the ways our resurrected Savior, for the next forty days, presented Himself alive by "many infallible proofs" and taught people about God's kingdom (Acts 1:3).

I turned to the last chapter of the books of John and Luke, immersing myself in some of Jesus' words during those last few weeks on earth. I imagined myself on the scene, following Him closely with pen and paper. (In the future, maybe I too could meet with Jesus in Galilee and attend a gathering of disciples. And maybe talk with Him, embrace Him, and ask Him questions!)

During my last few minutes of reading refreshment, I pored over Jesus' parting words before He ascended into heaven, when He gave His disciples the Great Commission (Matt. 28:19; Mark 16:15). This calling applies to us today as well.

Have you ever proclaimed the risen Christ—perhaps through a greeting card, a tract, or a group outreach? Have you ever presented to someone the historical evidence for the resurrection?[89] Consider the potential ramifications if you do so. For whoever responds to the Holy Spirit's conviction will be assured of heaven. And when the angels' announcement at the tomb—"He is risen!"—becomes a reality to them, they too can get drenched in His Word and filled with His everlasting joy.

> Blessed be the God and Father of our Lord Jesus Christ,
> who according to His abundant mercy has begotten us
> again to a living hope [of eternal life] through the
> resurrection of Jesus Christ from the dead.
> (1 Peter 1:3)

Taking Literal Steps of Faith

After completing a twelve-week course in personal witness training a while back, I wondered how I was going to share my faith in Christ as a lifestyle. I decided to start at a convalescent home where a friend of my dad's lived—expecting it to be less intimidating than striking up a conversation with a perfect stranger. When I parked my car and stepped out, it was a literal step of faith.

"Henry, do you remember me?" I asked with a cheerful smile when I saw him in the lobby.

"Oh, yes," he exclaimed. "You're Farmer John's daughter."

I stifled a giggle. My dad was often called Father John, but not Farmer John.

Henry asked me to push his wheelchair down the hall to his room for our visit, which I did. After chatting awhile, I raised the subject that burned on my heart. "Henry, I have a very important question to ask you. Have you ever said a prayer to receive Jesus as your personal Lord and Savior?"

"Well, I sure would," he said, "if I could ever forgive my son."

I assured Henry that God could give him the grace to forgive his son. When I offered to pray for God's grace, he accepted. So I did.

After I left, I wondered if I had been in tune with the Holy Spirit and said the right thing. It sure didn't fit the witnessing model I was taught. I didn't share any Scriptures or illustrations. I couldn't even remember any of them on the spot.

A few months later, I was in Henry's neighborhood, so I popped in to check on him. He told me he had talked to his son and they forgave each other! Then Henry told me he was ready to pray to receive Jesus Christ. We bowed our heads, and I led him in a prayer of salvation. Then I welcomed him into God's family with a big hug.

As I headed toward the door to leave, I glanced back and paused. Henry picked up the paperback Bible I had placed on his nightstand and started reading it. I sensed God's presence in that room.

Our Royal Redeemer not only brings us the victory of eternal life, as He did for Henry that day, He also brings us victories over our life issues. God gave Henry the grace to forgive his son, and

He gave me the grace to witness to Henry despite my fear of rejection. Jesus promised to accompany us whenever we share our faith (Matt. 28:20; Acts 1:8). And He did!

The next time you struggle with a life issue—such as forgiving someone or witnessing to someone—why not ask God to fill you with His (*agape*) love and enabling grace? Then trust that God's Spirit will lead and empower you. After all, God extends to believers the same exceedingly great power that "raised [Christ] from the dead" (Eph. 1:19–20). You might even sense God's presence—right there in the kitchen, or at a party, or in the office coffee-break room.

> I can do all things [God asks me to do]
> through Christ who strengthens me.
> (Phil. 4:13)

A splash of living water and apologetics

RESURRECTION VS. RESUSCITATION

Jesus' bodily resurrection from the dead was a unique miracle and the greatest feat in human history. By returning to life in His eternal body, Jesus Christ demonstrated that He had conquered death and sin.

All others who have returned to life were merely resuscitated or revived. Although their earthly lives were extended, eventually they physically died again[90]—including Lazarus, whom Jesus raised from the dead (John 11:43–44).

Jesus' miracle of bringing Lazarus back to life had tremendous significance. It foreshadowed His supreme miracle, it verified His claim to be the resurrection and the life (v. 25), and it demonstrated His power over the laws of nature.[91]

Believers will never experience spiritual death. Someday we will receive new glorified bodies—just as Jesus did—that won't be subject to death or decay. (See 1 Cor. 15:35–58.) Now, that's a profound truth we can celebrate forever!

A PROPHETIC PICTURE GOD PAINTED

For grand purposes unknown to Abraham, God instructed him to do something unthinkable. He asked Abraham to sacrifice his beloved son.[92] "Take now your son, your only son Isaac, whom you love, and go to the land of Moriah, and offer him there as a burnt offering on one of the mountains of which I shall tell you" (Gen. 22:2).

Naturally we'd expect Abraham to respond with some protest like, *But God, I waited twenty-five years for my promised son, Isaac. I don't want him to die so young!* Yet in complete dedication, this father of all true believers displayed one of the greatest acts of obedience known to man. He bound Isaac, placed him on an altar of wood on Mount Moriah, then lifted his knife to sacrifice his son.

Suddenly, the Angel of the Lord intervened! He called out from heaven and told Abraham to put down the knife, for he had passed the supreme test of faith[93] and demonstrated his heart of love for God (22:11–12). Instead of Isaac, a ram caught in the thicket became the burnt offering that day. To honor God for sparing his son, Abraham built an altar of worship. He called the place Jehovah Jireh—a declaration meaning "The Lord Will Provide" (22:8, 14).

We gain an insight into Abraham's thought process at the time of his intense testing by reading a passage in the Hebrews 12 "Hall of Faith." Abraham believed that if it became necessary, God would raise Isaac from the dead in order to carry out His word. For God had promised to produce a whole nation of descendants through Isaac (Heb. 11:18–19; see also Gen. 21:12).

In Genesis 22, God painted a prophetic mural for us on Mount Moriah. Abraham's poignant experience (c. 2000 BC) foreshadowed a momentous event to occur on the same mountain. Centuries later (c. AD 33), God the Father provided the ultimate sacrifice—His own beloved Son—to die in our place. John the Baptist identified Him as the "Lamb of God who takes away the sin of the world" (John 1:29).

As spiritual sons and daughters of Abraham, we too face challenging tests of faith in our lives. Here's one example: If an unbeliever inquires as to whether you're a Christian, will you take a stand and say yes? And will you avail yourself of that opportunity to express something wondrous about *Our Royal Redeemer*? If so, you will not only pass a test of faith, you will demonstrate that you worship the living God.

Hallelujah to the Father for His mega-sacrifice in sending Jesus. Hallelujah to the Son for enduring the cross in our place. What a merciful plan—prophesied in Scripture, portrayed in a living mural, and presented to us with endless love.

(Abraham said to Isaac:)
My son, God will provide for
Himself the lamb for a burnt offering.
(Gen. 22:8)

THE JOY OF THE LORD IS MY STRENGTH

Several years ago, a personal crisis rattled every nerve in my body. My son in the US Air Force was deployed to the Middle East. Donovan could be placed in harm's way. I feared he would be seriously injured in some military disaster. Or worse yet, I might never see him again! And since I didn't know whether he was a follower of Christ, his life could end without the security of heaven.

I asked nearly everyone I encountered to pray for Donovan's safety and salvation, and for me for relief from anxiety. Three long weeks after hearing the news of my son's deployment, God restored my peace and anchored my stirred-up emotions. The

Scripture verse that jumped off the page of my Bible and into my heart was Nehemiah 8:10, saying, "The joy of the Lord is your strength." I wasn't sure what that passage meant, so I looked into it.

In the context, a wave of Jews had just returned to Jerusalem after seventy years of captivity in Babylon. God raised up the prophet Nehemiah to help the people rebuild their city walls. Despite persistent opposition, the project took only fifty-two days and the children of Israel gladly moved back into their city.

On the first day of celebration, Ezra the priest read the scroll of the Law in the open square from morning until noon, leading the people in a spiritual revival. They worshipped God and wept when they heard the words of the Law (vv. 1–9). But Ezra encouraged them not to be dejected, for the day was sacred to God and the "joy of the Lord" could strengthen them (v. 10).[94]

No matter how serious my life issues are, I can experience joy by trusting in, and rejoicing in, the God of my salvation. And by recalling that He's the God of the big picture, who knows the end from the beginning. Unlike happiness, which depends on life's circumstances or people's moods, joy is a gladness of heart that can be constant for believers because God lives within us. The joy of the Lord is the source of our strength, so we need not allow the Enemy to rob us of our peace.

After considering those eight words of assurance in Nehemiah 8, I cast my cares upon the Lord (1 Peter 5:7) and my peace and joy returned.

Our Royal Redeemer loves Donovan and his family even more than I do, and I know He has faithfully watched over them for years. In fact, Donovan recently completed his military service, after being stationed in three different countries, attaining the rank of Master Sergeant.

Yet since a spiritual battle rages for the soul of every man, woman, and child, I will continue to pray for my son and his family, trusting that God will open the eyes of their hearts to see His greatness and know Him personally (Eph. 1:18).

Have life's struggles robbed you of your joy or peace recently? If so, be encouraged that God hears your prayers and is working behind the scenes. Spend some time reading the Word of God until you hear His words of assurance, and rejoice in the God of your salvation. If you are heartsick over the spiritual condition of a loved one, ask God to reveal to that person His gospel of grace and irresistible love. Then go your way, letting anxiety and sorrow be replaced by trust and joy.

> Do not sorrow [don't be sad and dejected],
> for the joy of the Lord is your strength.
> (Neh. 8:10)

MARY MAGDALENE'S DIVINE HERO

Mary from Magdala, a fervent follower of Jesus Christ, loved Him deeply. He had healed her, along with other women, of infirmities and evil spirits. And He became her divine Hero.

These women traveled with the disciples, sharing the good news about God's kingdom. For the King was in their very midst. They also contributed food and resources to support Jesus and His disciples (Luke 8:1–3).

Mary Magdalene's heart was heavy at the empty tomb on the third day following Jesus' burial. As she lingered there weeping, she looked inside the grave and saw two angels in white. When they asked why she was crying, she said she didn't know where her Lord had been taken. Then she turned around and saw Jesus. Supposing Him to be the gardener, she asked if He had carried away her Lord, and she offered to go get His body (John 20:11–15).

Imagine her surprise when her risen Savior called her by name. "Mary," He said, to which she replied, "Rabboni!" or Teacher (v. 16).

Not only was Mary the first person the Lord appeared to after His miraculous return to life, she was also the first person He commissioned to announce that He had risen from the dead—which she did (vv. 17–18). (See also Mark 16:9.)

Mary Magdalene's eyewitness testimony, memorialized in Scripture, has confirmed to countless people over the centuries that Jesus indeed returned to life. Hundreds of other observers, including the apostles, experienced the resurrected Jesus firsthand as well (see 1 Cor. 15:5–8).

One such remarkable encounter was the fried-fish breakfast Jesus had with seven disciples on the shore of the Sea of Tiberias. Although the fishermen had not caught a single fish the night before, Jesus advised them to cast their net on the right side of the boat. When they did, Peter had to drag the net to shore, containing 153 large fish (John 21:1–14).

Our Royal Redeemer ministers to our deepest needs, even unspoken ones. He rescued Mary from seven evil spirits, from her sin and spiritual separation from Him, and from her fear of losing Him.

As a believer, have you experienced the Lord's "TLC" in your life in countless ways? Because your major victory in life is knowing Jesus and having your name written in His Book of Life, you never need to fear losing your divine Hero. He loves to call you by name. He is preparing a heavenly mansion for you. And He treasures the personal moments you spend with Him in prayer. Have you met with your Redeemer lately and reciprocated His love?

(Our risen Savior said:)
I am He who lives, and was dead, and behold,
I am alive forevermore. Amen. And I have the keys
of [authority over] Hades and of Death.
(Rev. 1:18)

WORSHIPPING GOD FOR HIS AWESOM-AZING ATTRIBUTES

He is righteous (just), and He is/has wisdom.

Thank You, my loving Royal Redeemer, for saving me and issuing to me Your robe of righteousness to wear. Thank You for exchanging Your sinless life for my sin and its required punishment. You have declared me justified, and I will worship You and love You forever. Since You are the all-wise God, Your acts are all done in perfect wisdom—including atonement. As A. W. Tozer said, my part is not to explain it but simply to proclaim it.[95] Hallelujah, Lord! Thank You, amen.

THE TREASURED TRINITY

Reveals His Transcendent Love for Us

(A vision of Isaiah:)
I saw the Lord sitting on a throne, high and lifted up…
And one [seraphim-angel] cried to another and said:
"Holy, holy, holy is the Lord of hosts; the whole earth
is full of His glory!"…Also I heard the voice of the Lord,
saying: "Whom shall I send, and who will go for Us?"
(Isa. 6:1–3, 8)

Cinnamon Rolls in Outer Space

WHEN I GAZE at photos of spiral-shaped galaxies like the Milky Way—which to me resemble giant cinnamon rolls—I'm fascinated by their immensity, brilliance, and formations. They cause me to stand in awe of the maker of heaven and earth, who created them all.

In the words of Isaiah the prophet, the Creator measured the heavens with the span of His hand (Isa. 40:12). Just think. Since our great God has been around forever and made all things, He might have cast those spiral galaxies into space as easily as thrusting cinnamon rolls across the sky!

A few years ago, I attended an apologetics conference called "Understanding Intelligent Design."[96] At the end, a panel of professors fielded questions from the audience. My favorite question was this: "If only one percent of the planets appear to be earth-like and habitable, why did God create the universe so big?" The speakers offered two answers on the spot: (1) Since God's ways and thoughts are higher than ours (Isa. 55:8–9), He has lots of reasons for doing things that we don't understand. (2) Since God is big enough and has unlimited resources, He surely could have created our expansive universe and it wasn't wasteful of Him to do so.

While reviewing my conference notes, I thought of a third reason. With the benefit of time to reflect on that sky-high question, I considered this one a topper: The vast universe reveals to us glimpses of God's magnitude and magnificence, causing us to stand in awe of His creation and glory (Ps. 19:1).

However, a few weeks later when I shared these thoughts with my nephew, he added a fourth reason that brought me to my knees in praise and devotion: God created a wondrous place to have fellowship with man forever, and He has sovereignty over how He chooses to paint the fresco.

Wow! That explanation could provoke meditation that's deep and vivid. For we know from Scripture that God desires to have loving fellowship with us throughout eternity, and He designed the colors and rainbows. Perhaps our grand Creator drizzled colorful frostings on top of those dazzling cinnamon rolls to enhance the revolving artistry of heaven.

Although finite man is incapable of fully understanding infinite God, by studying Scripture we can glean glorious truths about Him, as well as glimmers of His majesty. The more diligently we study the Bible and pray, the more closely we can relate to our triune God—by conversing with the Father, in the name of Jesus, in the power of the Holy Spirit (Eph. 2:18).

Have you devoted yourself to meditating on God's Word? Are you engaging with our awesom-azing Lord in frequent prayer? If you make those things a priority, you will not only grow in spiritual truth, and be changed from the inside out, you will also bless the One whose love for you transcends all celestial boundaries.

> God is love. In this the love of God was [shown to us],
> that God has sent His only begotten Son into the
> world, that we might live through Him.
> (1 John 4:8–9)

ISAIAH'S GLIMPSE OF GOD

In a dramatic vision, Isaiah appeared in heaven's sanctuary and beheld the Lord in His magnificent glory (Isa. 6:1–8). Adonai sat on a throne that was high and lifted up, with the train of His robe filling the temple wall-to-wall. Mighty flying angels, called seraphim, covered their faces with two of their six wings as they worshipped God.

One seraph proclaimed God's glory and character by crying out, "Holy, holy, holy is the Lord of hosts; the whole earth is full of His glory!" (v. 3). Notice that the angel exclaimed *holy* three times. The repetition not only emphasizes the holiness of God, it is remarkably consistent with God's triunity. Commentator J. Vernon McGee suggests that it was a three-fold praise to the triune God: holy is the Father, holy is the Son, and holy is the Spirit.[97]

The temple foundations shook, and the sanctuary filled with smoke. Weak and frail—and keenly aware of his sinfulness—Isaiah said he was ruined. For his eyes beheld the holy King of creation. In contrast, Isaiah was a man flawed by sin, who dwelled with people of unclean lips (v. 5).

One of the mighty angels picked up a burning coal with tongs from the altar, then flew over to Isaiah and touched his lips with it. He pronounced Isaiah "not guilty," cleansed and forgiven. A marvelous spiritual transaction took place in Isaiah. For when he heard the Lord ask, "Whom shall I send, and who will go for Us?" he replied, "Here am I! Send me" (v. 8).

Notice that Adonai used the pronoun *Us,* indicating the plurality of persons within the Godhead.[98] Hence, Isaiah received his commission to be a prophet of almighty God—*The Treasured Trinity.*

Everyone in the body of Christ is called to some form of ministry. The Holy Spirit gives us spiritual gifts and abilities to use in serving our King. Your calling may be nothing like Isaiah's. Yours, for example, could be to lead musical worship, or teach the Bible, or join an evangelism team, or lead a prayer group. (See Rom. 12:6–8; 1 Cor. 12:4–11; Eph. 4:11.)

Have you asked the Lord how He wants you to partner with Him in building His kingdom? Remember, if He starts you out in a lowly position, He told us not to dislike the day of small beginnings because He rejoices to see the work begin (Zech. 4:10). In response to your own spiritual transaction with our mighty God, are you using your time for His glory? If not, consider praying, *Here I am, send me,* and then respond to Him readily and affirmatively as Isaiah did.

> I [Isaiah] heard the voice of the Lord, saying:
> "Whom shall I send, and who will go for Us
> [as a messenger to My people]?" Then I said,
> "Here am I! Send me."
> (Isa. 6:8)

MINING THE TREASURES OF GOD'S WORD

God spoke to my heart in an unforgettable way at an Anne Graham Lotz conference titled "Filling Up to Overflow," held at a nearby church.[99] Anne taught hundreds of Christian women how to study the Bible inductively by focusing on the first eight verses of Isaiah 6 (the passage we looked at in the previous devotion). She concluded the event by inviting attendees to stand for prayer if they were willing to devote themselves to giving out God's Word in our needy world—in effect, saying, "Here am I! Send me" (v. 8).

I'm in! I thought as I rose to my feet. As a daughter of the King, I was no longer a woman of unclean lips (v. 5), but righteous in Christ and forever grateful to Him.

When I looked around the sanctuary, I observed a wave of Christian sisters rising to their feet. It looked like every woman there responded to God's call. Having opened our hearts to His Word, we became inspired to mine its treasures and give out its more-priceless-than-gold words. Like Isaiah standing before the Lord of all creation, I believe many of us caught a fresh glimpse of the holy Trinity (v. 3). *God in three persons, blessed Trinity!*[100]

Not long after that conference, God airlifted me, figuratively, out of a store-front office where I distributed mail in exchange for free office space. Then He placed me in Bible college full time. Today, I am giving out the Word of God by speaking at women's events and writing gospel tracts, apologetics briefs, and devotionals.

I want people to know that the Bible—God's written revelation to mankind—is living, powerful, transforming, and eternal (Heb. 4:12; 1 Peter 1:23–25). "The words are empowered by God because they come with His authority and blessing. Wherever the Word of God is, the Spirit is present to make the words relevant, filled with power and life."[101]

Wherever those other conferees are today, I hope their hearts are still responding to the calling God gave them at the conference. I pray they are teaching God's Word, edifying the brethren and *sisteren* with it, and sharing its surpassing message that people can be cleansed and whole in Christ, and live with God forever.

Someday we will each see the spectacular throne room of God. Can you imagine what a joyful experience it will be to see our Lord clearly and hear Him speak to us audibly? (And I wouldn't be surprised if Jesus shows us which believers are in heaven partly because we shared His living Word with them.)

Lord, please continue to open my heart and mind to the riches of Your Word. Instead of merely scraping up a bit of gold dust by reading the Bible on a surface level, I want to dig deep and uncover nuggets of Your truth, instruction, love, and grace. Most of all, I want to know You more intimately and to catch greater glimpses of The Treasured Trinity.

> The word of God is living and powerful, and sharper
> than any two-edged sword, piercing even to the division
> of soul and spirit, and of joints and marrow, and is a
> discerner of the thoughts and intents of the heart.
> (Heb. 4:12)

A TWENTY-FOUR-HOUR PRAYER VIGIL

In the middle of the night, I drove on a dark, winding road to participate in a twenty-four-hour prayer vigil at my church in Indiana. My prayer partner Debbie, along with the pastors, organized the event to pray for salvations in the surrounding cities and for a revival in our land. Since not one prayer warrior had signed up to cover the 2:00 to 3:00 a.m. time slot, I received a special telephone invitation from her.

I accepted, considering it a calling from the Lord to pray in the middle of the night. As I drove toward the church, I sang the 1826 Trinitarian hymn "Holy, Holy, Holy"—partly to stay awake. After parking my car, I headed for the room with lights on. I sat on a chair positioned between the only two people there, Debbie and a cowboy.

To begin our prayer hour and prepare our hearts, my friend asked me to lead us in a worship song. The first song that came to mind was the hymn that kept my eyes open while driving over in the dark. So the three of us sang together:

Holy, holy, holy! Lord God Almighty!
Early in the morning our song shall rise to Thee.
Holy, holy, holy! merciful and mighty!
God in three persons, blessed Trinity![102]

"Now, that was an appropriate selection for two a.m.," Debbie exclaimed when we finished. "Early in the morning our song shall rise to Thee!" Getting to know my church family in Indiana was the highlight of my stay there for a year and a half. One standout blessing for me was joining that prayer vigil. The humble cowboy, who poured out his heart in prayer for lost souls (while most people were sleeping), left a lasting impression on me.

Sometimes I wonder whether he was an angel in disguise. He reminded me of Isaiah's vision, when the angels sang the same reverent refrain we did before the throne of God. Come to think of it, perhaps the three of us actually joined those seraphim in the middle of the night.

Do you enjoy expressing your heart of worship to the Lord in song? Next time you do, remember that you're in the very presence of our holy, merciful, mighty God, who inhabits the praises of His people (Ps. 22:3). How glorious it is that when we draw near to Him—no matter what time it is, day or night—He draws near to us (James 4:8).

One [seraphim] cried to another and said:
"Holy, holy, holy is the Lord of hosts;
the whole earth is full of His glory!"
(Isa. 6:3)

A splash of living water and apologetics

UNDERSTANDING THE CONCEPT OF THE TRINITY

While no symbol exists in the material universe that can adequately convey the Trinity (triunity of God), perhaps the nearest one is the Triquetra symbol displayed in this text box. It is made of one continuous line, representing the one eternal Godhead with three distinct Persons. The Bible teaches that all three personalities (the Father, Son, and Holy Spirit) are interconnected, sharing one divine essence.

(The Triquetra symbol was used by the early church to represent the Trinity, and it appears on many NKJV Bibles.)

* * *

It is essential to accept what is directly revealed in the Bible about the nature of God, rather than to read into the text what is not there to aid in human understanding.[103] When using sound biblical exegesis to interpret Scripture (as opposed to using eisegesis, which is subjective interpretation), we discover profound truths about the Trinity.

For example, as A. W. Tozer points out, Scripture reveals that all three persons of the Godhead are or were involved in the following:

- the work of creation

- the incarnation,

- the baptism of Christ,

- the atonement,

- the resurrection,

- an individual's salvation,

- and the indwelling of the Christian's soul.[104]

HEAVEN-SCENT PERFUME

Insecurity taunted me the week before I taught my first women's Bible study. My notes were prepared, and I was thrilled to have the opportunity to teach God's Word at a local church. However, I needed an engaging introduction—one that would express God's deep love for the women. So I petitioned God to show me an opening illustration that would not only break the ice, but confirm that He'd be present, inspiring me as I spoke.

To my relief, the Lord supplied the missing piece. Just two days before my speaking engagement, I smelled a sweet aroma coming from our upstairs guest room. *That's puzzling,* I thought. We hadn't had any recent guests, so no one had sprayed perfume in there. I popped my head around the corner to take a look. On the dieffenbachia house plant, I beheld a beautiful white magnolia-looking blossom emitting a fragrance I can only describe as "Heaven Scent."

Never before or after that day did the plant produce a blossom. In its glory days, the three-foot-tall plant stood stately with luscious green leaves. But it had degenerated into a scruffy shrub covered with brownish splotches, which I kept for sentimental reasons.

I shared with my Bible study sisters that we tend to think God's love for us is diminished when we disobey. From our human perspective, we think God is disappointed in us and rejects us when we fall or fail. If we buy into the Enemy's lie of condemnation, we will drift out of sweet fellowship with our Lord. Yet God's love for us is never lessened. And absolutely nothing can separate us from His love (Rom. 8:38–39).

We may see ourselves as scruffy, spotted plants before our holy God, but He sees us through Christ—in our already perfected state—as pure white, fragrant blossoms and delights in us.[105] Believers are declared innocent through the precious shed blood of Christ (1 Peter 1:18–19). And when we fall into sins daily, we have a *ready remedy* by accessing the 1 John 1:9 "spiritual bar of soap." When we honestly confess our sins, He forgives and cleanses us.

As children of the living God, what an honor it is to serve *The Treasured Trinity*, to appreciate His spectacular love, and to reflect on His mega-gift of salvation.

Abba Father, thank You for choosing me. And Jesus, thank You for redeeming me. And Holy Spirit, thank You for sealing me with Your presence as assurance of my future inheritance.[106] *I worship You, the holy triune God. I stand in awe of Your divine love for me because it is unconditional, and unbelievable, and unshakable.*

> Neither death nor life, nor angels nor principalities
> nor powers, nor things present nor things to come,
> nor height nor depth, nor any other created thing,
> shall be able to separate us from the love of
> God which is in Christ Jesus our Lord.
> (Rom. 8:38–39)

ENJOYING KOINONIA WITH GOD

Does it boggle your mind that the Ruler of the universe personally interacts with mere mortals? We can enjoy intimate fellowship (*koinonia* in Greek) with the divine Three-in-One. Although we can't wrap our minds around the concept of a God who's infinite and triune, we can wrap our arms around God through our loving relationship with Jesus. (See John 14:6; Gal. 2:20; Rev. 3:20.)

Based on his own experiences of walking with the Lord, John the apostle pleaded with believers to pursue joyful fellowship with Him (1 John 1:1–4). To help you picture John presenting his passionate appeal to you, consider this composite of verses he taught (in present-day wording):

> Beloved believers, please take notice! Truly we original apostles walked and talked with the Son of God, hearing, seeing, and touching Him. Based on our experiences

with Jesus and His divine teachings, we declare that you also can enjoy *koinonia* with the Father and with His Son, Jesus. You too can therefore be full of joy. We desperately desire that for you. You live in God and He lives in you by His Holy Spirit. Seriously consider God's extravagant love for you, for He calls you "children of God." Be sure to protect your close relationship with God, and let nothing take His place in your heart as number one. Amen.[107]

The apostle Peter also testified to the closeness the apostles had with Jesus. He declared that we can have inexpressible joy by loving and believing in Jesus, and that our reward for trusting Him will be our salvation (1 Peter 1:8–9). After witnessing Jesus' transfiguration (when His countenance changed and His face shown like the sun), Peter wrote this: "For we [apostles] did not follow cunningly devised fables when we made known to you the power and coming of our Lord Jesus Christ, but were eyewitnesses of His majesty" (2 Peter 1:16).

Are you pursuing *koinonia* with God through His Son? If so, surely you will enjoy firsthand experiences with Him as you journey through life together. You will also be able to wrap your mind and your arms a bit further around the majestic three-in-one God. And you might even find yourself presenting a passionate appeal to others to know (or to know even better) Jesus and His personal, extravagant love.

> Though now you do not see Him [Jesus], yet believing
> [and loving Him], you rejoice with joy inexpressible
> and full of glory, receiving the end [reward] of
> your faith—the salvation of your souls.
> (1 Peter 1:8–9)

THE MIRACLE OF REBIRTH

When my husband came to faith in Christ, he experienced the presence of our triune God in a unique way. Tom is a practical, no-nonsense guy with an engineering mind-set. Below is his own account of his marvelous transaction with God.

> God got my attention at a time of personal hardship, when everything important in my life had been stripped away: my kids, wife, job, bank account. My dad suffered a stroke. My brother broke his back.
>
> I felt a stirring in my heart from the Lord, so I stopped at a Christian bookstore and picked up a book. *How to Be Born Again* by Billy Graham just happened to be on sale that day. When I got home and started reading it on my patio, each question that popped into my mind about God was amazingly answered on the very next page. When I reached the end of the book, I got down on my knees and prayed the words on my heart.
>
> I said, "God, I've always been a self-sufficient, determined individual. If there was ever any goal to be accomplished or challenge to be met, I could do it. But now I know I need You. Please forgive me for my sins and be my Lord and Savior."
>
> Still kneeling on the cement porch, I glanced upward. I sensed God the Father's presence with me as Creator of the moon and stars and universe. As the sun warmed me, I felt embraced by Jesus, the Son of God. And as a gentle breeze brushed my cheeks, I felt the Holy Spirit there with me.
>
> For the very first time, I *experienced* God's divine love. My life changed forever by getting on course with my Redeemer. God is good!

The Treasured Trinity has made our eternal salvation possible. Surely it will take us—mere clumps of clay molded in the Potter's hand—countless ages to comprehend that glorious and mind-bending truth (Eph. 2:7). But for now, we can express to Him our heartfelt thanks.

Praises to the Father; praises to the Son; praises to the Holy Spirit for giving us life and rebirth. Thank You for the greatest miracle I could ever receive. Hallelujah!

[We were chosen] according to the foreknowledge
of God the Father, in sanctification of the Spirit,
[and cleansed by] the blood of Jesus Christ.
(1 Peter 1:2)

A splash of living water and apologetics

THE PREINCARNATE CHRIST CONFIRMS GOD'S THREE-IN-ONE NATURE

Theologian John F. MacArthur writes:

Keeping that in mind [that Christ was the Angel of the Lord in the Old Testament], it is then clear that there are several Old Testament passages where Christ is speaking, and in some of them He mentions two other divine persons. For example, in the book of Isaiah He says:

Come near to Me, listen to this:
From the first I have not spoken in secret,
    from the time it took place, I was there.
And now the Lord God has sent Me, and His Spirit.
(Isa. 48:16)[108]

* * *

The doctrine of the Trinity is a consistent and progressive teaching throughout the Bible. Consider, for example, the astounding Isaiah passage above.

Since technically the Bible isn't one single book, but rather a collection of sixty-six books written over fifteen centuries by forty authors, its amazing textual harmony and unity confirm its reliability and divine authorship. (See 2 Peter 1:21.)

OUR TRIUNE GOD WINS HEARTS

Some of the world's brightest minds today are wrestling with the mysteries of the holographic principle: how many dimensions are there in our universe? Some scientists in quantum physics say maybe four; others say perhaps eleven.[109] They just aren't sure. The subject of multidimensionality is so obscure to our human minds, we can only begin to grasp it through mathematical formulas. Even beyond that, consider the futility of people trying to understand the complexities of a transcendent Creator!

The wheels of my mind spin off their axis when I think about the wondrous ways of *The Treasured Trinity*. We are blessed indeed that our infinite God has chosen to reveal descriptions about Himself—through Scripture and the person of Jesus—that we otherwise could not know.

He also reveals astonishing and humbling truths concerning His relationship to us. Consider these, for example:

- Although God is holy, He loves sinners.

- Although God is almighty, He relates to us tiny creatures personally.

- Although God is lacking in nothing, He suffered deeply for us out of love.

- Although there is perfect interaction, love, and unity among the persons of the Trinity, God concerns Himself with fractured people in fractured relationships.

No wonder our awesom-azing God wins our hearts! He is greatly to be praised…and honored…and loved…and served…and spoken of…and treasured.

The next time you struggle to find words adequate to express worship to Him, consider turning to the book of Psalms for help. The psalms show us how great God is and how weak we are. Thirty of them have a thanksgiving theme. They praise God for

His gracious acts, remind us of His blessings, and give us grateful hearts.[110]

To enrich your relationship with our awesom-azing God, why not ask the Holy Spirit to inspire you to create your own psalms to glorify Him? Or, as one Bible commentator suggests, "Ask God to show you how to give all of yourself to the acts of praise and worship… Simply bring Him that obedient attitude and ask Him to teach you how to worship with all your heart, soul, mind, and strength."[111] After all, He desires and deserves our utmost worship. For His excellent name is multi-dimensional.

> Our Lord, how excellent is Your name in all the earth…
> When I consider Your heavens, the work of Your fingers,
> the moon and the stars, which You have ordained,
> what is man that You are mindful of him?…
> You have crowned him with glory and honor.
> (Ps. 8:1–5)

OUR TRANSACTION WITH A BANK TELLER

One afternoon Joanie (my friend who loves to share Jesus) stopped at my bank with me so I could withdraw some cash. Since no customers waited in line, I filled out my transaction paperwork at the teller window. Recognizing a window of opportunity, Joanie engaged the tall, dark-skinned man behind the counter (I'll call him Armeen) in casual conversation.

"My daughter used to work at this bank," she said, breaking the ice. Upon noticing his name badge, she asked, "Is your name Persian?"

When he confirmed that it was, Joanie asked him if Persians believe in Jesus.

Armeen responded that some of them do. Then he mentioned he had recently become a Jehovah's Witness.

Handing him my withdrawal slip, I said in a caring voice, "I wish you were a born-again Christian."

"You know, I've been talking to a lot of Christians lately," he replied. "They've tried to explain the Trinity, but it just doesn't make sense to me."

While I tried to balance both my financial figures and my spiritual thoughts, Joanie responded. "Do you think it's possible to fully understand how God created the universe?"

"No way!"

"Well, neither can we fully understand the concept of the Trinity. It's a marvelous mystery."

"Actually," I added, "if God were small enough for us understand, He wouldn't be big enough to worship, right?"

"Interesting point." The teller smiled, handing me cash and a withdrawal receipt. As we turned to leave, he gave us a cordial nod.

Later that day, I mailed Armeen a thank-you note for his friendly and efficient service and enclosed an apologetics tract about the Trinity.[112] Since I rarely go inside my bank, I never saw Armeen again. However, my girlfriend and I prayed that God would open his spiritual eyes and that someday he'd make a personal transaction with our triune God.

If my bank teller does become a believer, he will have more riches than any bank could ever hold. Although he still wouldn't be able to comprehend our three-in-one God, at least he'd know that He is a Father who loves him, a Son who died for him, and a Spirit who comforts him.[113] And if he becomes a devoted follower, pursuing Jesus as a special jewel, he will be the beneficiary of untapped treasures of wisdom and knowledge (Col. 2:2).

Why not set that worthwhile goal for yourself? God desires for all believers to become diligent disciples who grow in the grace and knowledge of our Lord and Savior (2 Peter 3:18). If you do, you will surely derive endless dividends.

[I, Paul, have agonized in prayer for the brethren to grow
in love and in] the knowledge of the mystery of God
[in whom lies] all the treasures of wisdom and knowledge.
[Christ is the reservoir of all knowledge.[114]]
(Col. 2:1–3)

GOD'S INFINITE LOVE FOR US

Whenever I meditate on John chapter 17, it feels as if I am standing on holy ground. While all Scripture is divinely inspired, in this passage we are privy to the intimate prayers Jesus spoke to God the Father, just hours before He approached the cross. In addition to praying from the depths of His soul for His disciples and for Himself, Jesus prayed for all believers (vv. 20–26). He ended His prayer by declaring the great secret of Christian living—"Jesus and His love indwelling the believer."[115]

After this time of prayer, Jesus and His followers crossed the Kidron Ravine and entered Gethsemane, an olive grove. Knowing what was going to occur there, Jesus made Himself available to His enemies. A battalion of Roman soldiers and temple guards arrested Him (18:1–12). As prophesied, the Lamb of God proceeded to the slaughter without resistance (Isa. 53:7).

We cannot comprehend the love Jesus demonstrated by dying for all humanity while we were His enemies (Rom. 5:8). Neither can we grasp how much it cost the Lord of glory to atone for our sins. Michael Card presents an endearing portrayal of this in his book *Violent Grace*:

> Jesus Christ is God's Lamb for you and me. And as we come to the cross, let us come humbly, laying trembling hands upon the Lamb. He will hear us whisper [to Him] through our tears: "What happened to You, Lord Jesus, should have happened to me."[116]

We believers are blessed indeed, for our Savior carried out God's universe-reverberating plan for us. Then Jesus called out to each of us, *I love you with an infinite love. I gave My life for you. Trust in Me for your salvation. Choose life!* And we responded to His invitation. Now that Jesus and His perfect love reside in us (John 17:26), we can actually experience the kind of love the members of the Trinity share with one another.

In light of God's infinite love—for you and within you—are you ready to draw even closer to Him? The next time you celebrate the sacrament of communion, why not spiritually place your trembling hands upon the Lamb of God and whisper words of gratitude to Him for taking your place? By doing so, you will be remembering that His body was broken for you and His blood was shed for you (1 Cor. 11:24–25). You will also be sharing the divine love experienced by the Father, Son, and Holy Spirit.

(Jesus prayed to God the Father:)
That the world may know that You have sent Me,
and have loved them as You have loved Me…I have
declared to them Your name, and will declare it, that the love
with which You loved Me may be in them, and I in them.
(John 17:23–26)

WORSHIPPING GOD FOR HIS AWESOM-AZING ATTRIBUTES

He is triune within His unity, and He is/has immortality.

Dear God, You are the treasure that I seek, and I marvel over Your majesty. Although I can't wrap my mind around Your infinite, triune nature, I thank You that I can wrap my arms around You through my relationship with Jesus. Thank You for Your abundant love. I love You because You first loved me. Thank You for writing my name in the Lamb's Book of Life and for giving me an inheritance with You. I praise and worship You, The Treasured Trinity—the Father, the Son, and the Holy Spirit. In Jesus' holy name, amen.

THE GOD OF ALL TRUTH

BLESSES US WITH GENUINE TRUTH

(Jesus prayed to God the Father:)
Sanctify them by Your truth. [Set My believers
apart for Your special use.] Your Word is truth.
(John 17:17)

SHOWCASED FOR ALL TO SEE

AS MY HUSBAND and I drove home from a family wedding in Las Vegas, I spotted a large billboard along the highway. The entire sign was blank except the bold citation—*Revelation 1:7.* Right there in the dry, 110-degree desert heat of August was an announcement of living water for thirsty souls. Out in that sandy wasteland was the Lord's signature of truth, showcased for all to see!

Could that Scripture be an answer to my prayer? I wondered as I reached for the miniature Bible in my briefcase and looked up the verse. Revelation 1:7 announces that Jesus "is coming with clouds, and every eye will see Him." It was no coincidence that this sign captured my attention. I had been praying for weeks for the meant-to-match Scripture for this devotion. And there it was, boldly towering over Interstate 15.

According to that Revelation passage, Jesus Christ, the Logos (the incarnate Word),[117] will return to earth someday. Everyone will know His identity because they will see Him "coming with clouds" (v. 7). When *The God of All Truth* appears, truth will prevail. He will silence all contrary voices of distortion, dishonesty, and distrust.

At the ascension of Christ on the mountain in Galilee, two men in white apparel, presumably angels, prophesied of Jesus' return. They declared to the apostles, as Jesus ascended in a cloud, "Men of Galilee, why do you stand gazing up into heaven? This same Jesus, who was taken up from you into heaven, will so come in like manner as you saw Him go into heaven [in a cloud]" (Acts 1:11).

Shortly before His crucifixion, Jesus Himself announced that He would come back on the "clouds of heaven with power and great glory" (Matt. 24:30; see also Luke 21:27).

Hopefully that highway billboard I saw in the desert will catch the attention of many travelers who will be curious enough to get out a Bible and take heed that Jesus is returning. I pray they will recognize the Lord's signature highlighted on every page they read, and that the Holy Spirit will quicken their hearts to God's truth. Then more thirsting souls will find living water to quench their long-lasting thirst before it's too late.

Are you doing your part to further God's truth? We have a limited time in which to do so—through the Spirit-led words we speak, the actions we take, and the lives we live. Why not ask the Holy Spirit to refill you (Eph. 5:18) throughout the day so you can influence others toward spiritual truth? If you do, surely more Christ-rejecters will become Christ-accepters, and more believers will prepare to worship the King face-to-face.

When Jesus finally arrives, He will be showcased for all to see—victoriously, yet with scarred hands and feet. Many will rejoice…many will mourn…and truth will no longer be clouded.

> Behold, [Jesus] is coming with clouds, and every
> eye will see Him, and they also who pierced Him.
> And all the tribes of the earth will mourn
> because of Him. Even so. Amen.
> (Rev. 1:7)

FORGING AHEAD FULL SPEED

In his excellent book *Faith,* Pastor Chuck Smith uses the analogy of a boat with two oars to explain that in order to mature in Christ, our faith and works must operate together. Christians need to focus on both, because faith empowers our works, and works prove our faith.[118] Rowing with a single oar cannot transport a boat across the lake, because the boat will spin in circles and not move forward. We need two oars to successfully reach our goal.

As a variation of this analogy, consider this salvation scenario. A boater desires to journey to the opposite side of a large lake, and numerous boats are available. To do so, first he needs to select the one-and-only boat that is structurally capable. Second, he must connect the motor to his boat to propel it forward.

Likewise, an unbeliever who desires to reach heaven must first select the true and living God, who alone is able to carry him there. If he falls for false teachings and chooses an inadequate god, he will sink spiritually. A cultist, for example, may be sincere in his faith yet sincerely wrong in his view of God (see Rom. 10:2–4). Our faith is only as valid as the object of our faith—which must be the biblical Jesus.

Second, the unbeliever must decide to trust in the true God. Those who know about Jesus Christ, yet never act on their faith by connecting with Him in a personal relationship, will never arrive in heaven. It is possible for a person to intellectually agree that Jesus is the divine Son of God (which trembling demons believe, according to James 2:19) yet procrastinate or refuse to receive Jesus as his Savior. As a result, his boat will drift endlessly.

Nothing in life compares to embracing *The God of All Truth*, the Lover of our souls. Nothing comes close to the peace of mind and security that comes from knowing He will greet us when we reach heaven's shore. Our awesom-azing God freely offers everyone safe passage to heaven, and He instructs us to pray for our fellow travelers to embrace that truth as well.

Do you keep a list of unbelievers and pray for them regularly? Do you pray that God will open their spiritual eyes to the gospel of grace (2 Cor. 4:4) so they can recognize their need to call on Jesus? If you do, some of them may get on board with *The God of All Truth*. Then they will forge ahead full speed—with no desire to look back at the world that soon will pass away (1 John 2:17).

> For by grace you have been saved through faith
> [in Jesus Christ], and that not of yourselves; it is the
> gift of God, not of works, lest anyone should boast.
> (Eph. 2:8–9)

FELLOW WORKERS FOR THE TRUTH

The spiritual battle over truth heated up in the heavenlies during the first century. Spirit-led disciples spread God's Word and gospel of grace, thereby "turning the world upside down" (Acts 17:6). Yet right on their heels, false teachers circulated error. They disputed the apostles' teachings and tried to diminish Jesus' identity.

To correct heresy, John the apostle wrote three epistles on the vital themes of truth and love. In 1 John, he presented a clear picture of Christ and His incarnation, warning believers about antichrists who deny the deity of Christ. He also highlighted the importance of loving God (through obedience) and loving each another.

In 2 John, the apostle taught that God's truth never changes and it lives in our hearts forever (v. 2). John exhorted home-fellowship churches to protect and promote God's revealed Word, to love one another, and to reject false teachings. He also gave them a warning: if believers became influenced by deceivers, they risked forfeiting their full reward from the Lord Himself some-day (v. 8). And if they wandered beyond Christ's teachings, no longer abiding in the "doctrine of Christ," they would not have God (v. 9).[119]

In 3 John, the apostle emphasized the importance of walking in truth and serving the brethren in love. To illustrate, he contrasted two church leaders—faithful Gaius and faithless Diotrephes. While Gaius walked in truth and displayed loving servanthood, Diotrephes walked in error and displayed selfishness. He even rejected John's apostolic authority and refused to receive the missionaries whom John sent out.[120] In contrast, Gaius showed love and hospitality to those ministers, for which John commended him as one of the "fellow workers for the truth" (v. 8).

The God of All Truth is well pleased when believers work together for truth. When we believe the essential doctrines of the Christian faith and share God's Word in love (Eph. 4:15), we reach the lost and edify the brethren. We also leave legacies to our loved ones when we study our Bibles diligently, serve the Lord gladly, and walk with Him faithfully.

Are you advancing God's truth in today's mixed-up world, ever mindful that countless people are deceived and going astray? Are you serving the brethren in Christ's love? If so, you are a partner for the truth, a vessel of God whose faithful service is helping to turn the world upside down—or right side up—for Christ.

We therefore ought to [love and support our
missionary-minded brethren who go forth for the
Lord] that we may become fellow workers for the truth.
(3 John 8)

A splash of apologetics to share

THE ULTIMATE TRUTH WAR

The kingdom of darkness battles intensely against the kingdom of light over people's souls. Satan, the grand conspirator, employs two age-old strategies to diminish truth: attacking the validity of the Word of God and discrediting the gospel. Beginning in the garden, he tempted Eve with *Did God really say?* (Gen. 3:1; see also 2 Tim. 3:15; Rev. 12:9).

However, despite efforts by the devil and his fallen angels to distort truth, our Creator-God has revealed to us that He is the source of all truth; the Scriptures are our basis for truth; and Jesus Christ, the Word incarnate, *is* the truth.

Over the centuries, the forces of darkness have attempted to nullify the Bible, and to thwart God's promises for humanity, by cutting off the messianic line (e.g., see Est. 3:13 and Gen. 6:1–8 and Matt. 2:12–18). For if the chosen line were destroyed, then God's plan to send the Savior of the world and to judge Satan would be prevented.

But our mighty God always wins. In His perfect timing, *The God of All Truth* will overcome all evil and deception. And the word of God is forever settled in heaven (Ps. 119:89).

* * *

Postmodernism (a major strategy to diminish truth) asserts that all truth is based on perspective and our access to reality requires interpretation. So it would be impossible to understand what God would intend to reveal to us.

However, as apologist Ravi Zacharias keenly points out, "Ought not the Supreme Being be able to reveal His truth to those of *every* tongue and tribe, regardless of its context?"[121]

A Divine Appointment
at the Mall

I've only encountered a couple of people who got upset when I witnessed to them about Jesus—and I learned from it. One of them was a young man I'll refer to as Maxwell, a salesman who sold cell phones and telephone service contracts at the mall. My witnessing partner and I chatted with him while no shoppers showed up.

When Maxwell told us he was a Catholic, I wondered whether he understood the difference between religion and relationship. In my own life, understanding that distinction was a turning point, coming from my background of legalism. As we discussed that matter, Joanie pointed out that we actually *knew* Jesus personally. She also shared the wonderful reality that since He paid the full price for our salvation, there was no need to try earning it.

Anger flashed in Maxwell's eyes. "Are you saying that because I'm a Catholic I'm not going to heaven?"

I gave him a friendly smile. "Not at all. We're just suggesting that you read John chapter 3 in your Bible and see what Jesus says about being born again."

Immediately his fierce gaze softened. He even agreed to read the Bible passage that night after work.

As Joanie and I turned to leave, I reminded him, "John chapter 3!"

He nodded.

My friend and I headed down the corridor. "That was a good example of how a soft answer turns away wrath," she said, referring to Proverbs 15:1.

I agreed. Perhaps Maxwell could tell that we viewed him through the loving eyes of Jesus, as someone for whom He died. (I sure hope so!) Or maybe he was under the Holy Spirit's conviction, which sometimes causes an unbeliever to respond negatively because God is speaking to him and he's fighting against Him.[122]

Joanie and I prayed that Maxwell would follow through and read John 3, with an open heart. We asked the Lord to reveal His love and illuminate His truth to him. What a thrill to think that the Holy Spirit might have worked through our brief witness at the cell-phone kiosk in the mall.

Aren't you grateful that Jesus revealed to Nicodemus, and to us, that unless someone is reborn, he or she cannot see the kingdom of God (John 3:3)? And that whoever believes in Him will not perish but have everlasting life (3:16)? All praise and honor to our God! For by His grace, He has prepared a way for fractured people to become whole again. He plans to bless us forever with His love, His presence, and His truth. And Jesus promises that whoever comes to Him will by no means be cast out (John 6:37).

(Jesus Christ declared:)
Most assuredly, I say to you, unless one is
born again, he cannot see the kingdom of God.
(John 3:3)

THE ISLAND OF CORRUPTION

I shudder to think about the utter hopelessness of humanity if *The God of All Truth* had not revealed Himself to us. What if Jesus had never come for us?

I'm reminded of the allegorical novel *The Lord of the Flies*, written by William Golding in 1954. The movie adaptation left a lasting impression on me. The plot involves several British schoolboys, ages six to twelve, who survive a plane crash during wartime and take refuge on a jungle island in the South Pacific.

At the outset, the boys form a society and attempt to live together peacefully with some sense of order. As time goes by, however, they degenerate into barbaric, bloodthirsty hunters who turn on one another. One boy realizes a dark secret: the imaginary beast they all fear (the beast of savagery) exists within each of them. As their fears intensify, the boys offer sacrifices to a dead beast, treating it as a tribal god. This "Lord of the Flies" (in Greek, *Beelzebub*) is a decapitated pig's head that attracts flies as it decomposes.

The story ends when Ralph, one of the leaders, runs for his life and falls on the beach. As he looks up, he sees a British naval officer who had just arrived. Ralph breaks down and cries, presumably from his colliding emotions of trauma, fear, and relief. In the distance, a cruiser waits to return any survivors to civilization.

In this allegory, the boys' corrupt island represents the adult world of corruption. According to author Golding, his theme traces the defects of society back to the defects of human nature—the darkness of man's heart. Even the naval officer at the end of the story is a hunter who is "enmeshed in the same evil as the symbolic life of the children on the island."[123]

Golding's theme aligns with biblical truth: left to our own, the human condition is degenerate. Our souls are separated from God, and our hearts are desperately wicked (Jer. 17:9). The Grand Rescue for us occurred when the sinless Son of God humbly came to earth in human form, then died on the cross to atone for our sins. Our part is merely to receive the Savior—freely climbing aboard the rescue ship to eternal safety.

Hallelujah to The God of All Truth! Thank You for showing me the truth about my human condition. Thank You for revealing to me Your sacrificial love. And thank You for permanently rescuing me from my own island of corruption. For there is no other Savior!

Jesus Christ, who, being in the form of God,...made Himself of no reputation, taking the form of a servant, and coming in the likeness of men,...humbled Himself and became obedient to the point of death, even the death of the cross.

(Phil. 2:5–8)

LOVE WITHIN THE CONTEXT OF TRUTH

Definitions of *love* abound. Our culture defines it in unlimited ways, especially in our postmodern world that embraces relative truth. Love, however, is to be understood and exercised within the boundaries of biblical truth or else we sacrifice truth. We aren't walking in love when we wink at false doctrine or help people to undermine truth.[124]

Commentator J. Vernon McGee explains the relationship between love and truth, as taught by the apostle John (in 2 John 5–6):

> Love and truth are inseparable. Christ is the epitome of both; He is the incarnation of both. He is the Truth (John 14:6), and He is love (1 John 4:16). When truth and love are in contrast and conflict, which one should prevail? The apostle John's startling reply is that truth comes first. Love can be expressed only within the bounds and context of truth—only within the limitation and boundary that Scripture sets.[125]

Consider the harm that's caused when love is practiced outside the context of truth: unleashed lust, deteriorating families, confused youth, turmoil in society, eventual chaos.

John urges believers, then and now, "to love one another" as we have heard from the beginning in God's commandments (2 John 6). Based on our close walk with God and the Holy Spirit's empowering, we can love the brethren with God's *agape* love (described in 1 Cor. 13:4–8; see also Gal. 5:16, 22).

As for people outside the faith, God asks us to show them His extraordinary love primarily by taking the gospel to them. We could let them know that one of God's attributes is pure love, and that His love has provided a Savior for us.[126] Or point out that although our human tendency is to believe that man's greatest need is love, the Bible clearly teaches that man's greatest need is a

Savior. And by receiving Jesus—the Savior of the world—we will enjoy both ultimate Love and ultimate Truth.

Are you ready to heed God's call to love one another within the context of truth? To do so might require re-prioritizing your goals in life. But if you do, you will please the Lord, which is the highest aim for a child of God. You will fit into Jesus' plan as He builds His church. And others will realize that you're a follower of Christ—who is perfect Love and Truth.

> Now I plead with you,…that we love (*agape*)
> one another. This is love, that we walk
> [in truth] according to His commandments.
> (2 John 5–6)

A splash of living water and apologetics

RELATIVE TRUTH AND TOLERANCE

In today's postmodern world that promotes relativism, it is politically incorrect to say there is only one way to heaven. The unpopular mega-message—that everyone needs Jesus as their Savior—is often minimized or criticized.

According to the new-tolerance mentality, no one is wrong in his or her religious or moral views, so people need to treat all faiths as equal. Yet this mind-set is *logically inconsistent* because it rejects one view: its proponents (the relativists) are intolerant toward those who believe in objective truth and morality.[127]

Christians are called to take a stand for biblical truth and share it with others in love, even in the face of rejection. We can also pray for unbelievers' spiritual illumination. For when God waters the seeds of truth in their hearts, they might call on our Redeemer—who faced the ultimate rejection, on their behalf. (See Isa. 55:11; John 4:36–38.)

> It is encouraging to know that there are always people ripe and ready to respond to *The God of All Truth*. And those who drink of the living water of God's gospel will be eternally grateful.
>
> * * *
>
> We are cruel to ourselves if we try to live
> in this world without knowing about the God
> whose world it is and who runs it.[128]
> —J. I. Packer

PRESERVED FROM RELIGIOUS PITFALLS

Have you ever thanked *The God of All Truth* for preserving you from falling into religious pitfalls that twist truth and snag souls? Because they are widespread, you might have passed through such traps before our merciful God called you out (1 Peter 2:9) and you heeded His voice (John 10:27). Praise God, as sons and daughters of the King, we are positioned on the victorious side of the invisible battle for truth. We know Yahweh!

Naturally, we've all encountered salvation delays or detours in our journeys through life. Several of my close friends and relatives have fallen prey to religious deceit—including my stepdad, my girlfriend's husband, my dentist, my high school classmate, my ex-fiancé, and my next-door neighbor. I continue to pray for them, that their spiritual blindness is only temporary and that someday I will see them in heaven.

Were it not for the grace of God, some of the people who have come into my life might have persuaded me to fall into counterfeit spirituality or errant theology. Isn't that true for you as well?

Sooner or later, all gurus, gods, and idols will fall on their faces. Only the true God will stand. As King Solomon prayed when he dedicated the newly built temple to Him, "Even the highest heavens cannot contain you… May people all over the earth know that the Lord is God and that there is no other god" (1 Kings 8:27, 60 NLT).

Jesus Christ—*The God of all Truth*—wants people to know that He was condemned to set us free. As Michael Card points out, in the book of John, Jesus made these powerful statements about truth:

- To Nicodemus: "I tell you the truth, no one can see the kingdom of God unless he is born again" (3:3).

- Teaching in the temple courts: "He who works for the honor of the one who sent him is a man of truth; there is nothing false about him" (7:18).

- To His new converts: "You will know the truth, and the truth will set you free" (8:32).

- To an angry mob: "You are determined to kill Me, a Man who has told you the truth that I heard from God" (8:40).

- To His anxious disciples: "I am the way and the truth and the life" (14:6).

- To Pilate during His own trial: "For this reason I was born, and for this I came into the world, to testify to the truth. Everyone on the side of truth listens to Me" (18:37).[129]

Abba Father, thank You for preserving me from religious pitfalls. I'm grateful that Your Holy Spirit opened my eyes to see the Savior of the world and illuminated the Scriptures to my heart and mind. Now I am destined for heaven. And I can testify to others about the true God, who stands ready to ensure their salvation too. In Jesus' priceless name I pray, amen.

Lead me in Your truth and teach me,
for You are the God of my salvation; on You
I wait all the day [putting my hope in You].
(Ps. 25:5)

FIVE SURPRISED FISHERMEN

The summer I handed out tracts to five fisherman in Fort Collins, Colorado, I'm not sure who was more surprised—them or me.

I was participating in a conference sponsored by Campus Crusade for Christ International. They had invited True-Way Tracts, my ministry, to sponsor a resource table in their bookstore. I was grateful for the opportunity to offer our apologetics pamphlets, which promote and defend the truth of Christianity.

Early one morning before the event—wearing a jogging suit, tennies, and a visor—I went for a nature walk around the lake. As I headed back to my rental car, I spotted five older fellows holding fishing gear and chatting as they leaned against their van.

The idea came to my mind to witness to them about Jesus before they took off. I gained a bit of courage by reminding myself that my permanent citizenship is in heaven and that I'm just a sojourner passing through this life (Phil. 3:20). However, a canceling thought came immediately. *You can't do that. You haven't done your daily devotions yet.*

I sat in the driver's seat, deliberating in a mental tug-of-war. I concluded that if I didn't act soon, the fishermen and the opportunity would be gone. So I asked the Lord to lead me. Then I grabbed a variety of tracts out of my briefcase and approached the men.

"Hello, there," I said with a gentle boldness. "I was born in Colorado, but now I live in California."

They stared at me with expressionless faces, as if to say, *And who cares about that?*

"I'm a Christian writer. Are any of you Christians?"

After a long pause, one fisherman said, "I go to church."

Another stated, "I'm a Christian."

I handed that fellow all five of my tracts. "Then you might want to share these with your friends. They contain the message of Jesus." I pointed to one apologetics tract. "This one, for example, gives evidence to show that Jesus actually rose from the dead."

Sensing it was time to leave, I retreated to my car. As I pulled away, I turned to wave farewell. But none of the fishermen looked up because they were busy reaching for tracts.

Smiling, I prayed not only that God would water the seeds of His truth in their hearts, but that He would make them "fishers of men" (Matt. 4:19).

Have you ever experienced a mental tug-of-war when an opportunity came to share the truth about Jesus? Next time that happens, don't wait until you do your daily devotions, or finish eating breakfast, or change out of your exercise clothes. Ask the Lord to lead you, then go for it! Even if you're rejected, *The God of All Truth*, who is with you, will be pleased. After all, He was despised and rejected by men—for you, for me, and for everyone (Isa. 53:3).

(Jesus declared to His disciples:)
[Surely] I am with you always,
even to the end of the age.
(Matt. 28:20)

A splash of living water

EVERY KNEE WILL BOW

Three times in the Bible we are told that someday, at the mighty name of Jesus, every knee shall bow and every tongue shall confess that Jesus Christ is Lord (Rom. 14:11; Phil. 2:10–11; see also Isa. 45:23). All creation will recognize His superiority.

Everyone will give an account of himself (or herself) at the judgment seat of Christ (Rom. 14:10–12). Those who received Him as their Savior during their lifetimes will enter heaven and receive rewards (see 1 Cor. 3:12–15). For those who haven't, it will be too late to receive salvation.[130]

Tragically, those who die without Christ will be consigned to an eternity apart from God. Although they will acknowledge Jesus' lordship, it will not be a confession to salvation but to condemnation for rejecting God's Son.[131]

Accordingly, let's diligently pray for lost souls to respond to God's love, gospel, and truth. Then when that day of determination arrives, more people will be gladly praising our conquering King on bended knee.

* * *

To give truth to him who does not
love the truth is to only give more
reasons for misinterpretation.[132]
—George MacDonald

PAUL'S TRIAL BEFORE KING AGRIPPA

Consider the apostle Paul's anointed self-defense when tried before King Agrippa in Caesarea (Acts 26:1–29). Paul's evangelistic efforts had created a serious controversy. The legal charges against him were dissension among the Jews and rebellion against Roman rule. However, the Lord turned the Enemy's opposition into an opportunity for Paul to preach.

Here is Paul's opening statement: "I think myself happy, King Agrippa, because today I shall answer for myself before you concerning all the things of which I am accused by the Jews…" (v. 2). In presenting his case, Paul included his conversion testimony, God's good news, and a powerful apologetic on Jesus' resurrection.

In response, Festus, the governor of Judea, accused Paul of being mad.

"I am not mad, most noble Festus," replied Paul, "but [I] speak the words of truth and reason" (v. 25).

Paul then turned to King Agrippa and asked him if he believed the prophets. Although touched by Paul's words, the king replied, "You almost persuade me to become a Christian" (v. 28). Upon deliberating with Festus, Agrippa concluded that Paul had done nothing worthy of death or chains (v. 31).

Bible commentator Jon Courson challenges us, when we encounter spiritual opposition, to follow Paul's example of seizing the opportunity:

> Agrippa saw Paul's trial as a mistake. Paul, however, used it as an opportunity to share the gospel. So, too, in whatever trial you face, may God give you grace to say, "Happily I stand here today knowing this is an opportunity for me to share something of my faith and something of His [Jesus'] life."[133]

Recently, one of my "prayer sisters" appeared before small-claims court concerning a landlord-tenant disagreement. In advance, we prayed that God would use her as a witness for Him—and He did. She not only waived her right to countersue, she shared seeds of God's truth and kindly told people that Jesus loved them.

As a sold-out-for-Jesus apostle, Paul longed for countless lost souls to know *The God of All Truth*. No wonder Paul asked the brethren to pray for him for boldness to make known the mystery of the gospel (Eph. 6:19).

Although not all believers are evangelists, we all can use our giftings to advance the gospel. Why not, for example, ask the Holy Spirit to lead you in your posts, e-mails, or casual conversations to "speak the words of truth and reason." Then be alert for a chance to share a truth about Jesus, a personal testimony, a

Christian apologetic, and/or the saving gospel. After all, no door is too heavy for God to open—including doors of opportunities.

(Paul testified:)
Having obtained help from God, to this day I stand,
witnessing both to small and great, saying [things prophesied
by Moses and the prophets] that the Christ would
suffer, that He would be the first to rise from the dead, and
would proclaim light to the Jewish people and to the Gentiles.
(Acts 26:22–23)

BAAL VS. YAHWEH, THE LIVING GOD

Wouldn't you love to see a show-down between Yahweh and today's pagan gods? To witness a challenge between the living God and pretend gods? I'd appreciate seeing an event similar to the "Which God is really true?" contest that the prophet Elijah called on Mount Carmel (1 Kings 18:19–40).

At the time, Jezebel, the wife of King Ahab, had attempted to obliterate the worship of Yahweh and instead make Baal (the popular Canaanite god) the official god of Israel. While the Israelites wavered in their loyalties, Elijah warded off the crisis.

As the only remaining prophet of the Lord, he single-handedly challenged 450 prophets of Baal to a test: would Baal or Yahweh answer by fire, proving to be the true God? On Mount Carmel, two bulls cut into pieces were laid over wood on two altars—one for Baal and one for Yahweh.

The unreal god, Baal, made no reply when his prophets shouted to him for hours. The deceived men only met silence. However, when Elijah prayed to the God of Abraham, Isaac, and Jacob, the fire of Yahweh fell and consumed the burnt sacrifice—plus the wood, the stones, and the dust, and even evaporated the water in the surrounding trench.

Upon witnessing this miracle, the people of Israel fell on their faces proclaiming, *The Lord, He is God! The Lord, He is God!* (v. 39).

The counterfeit credentials of pagan gods and idols will fall foolishly short when compared to Yahweh, who declares that He will not share His glory with anyone (Isa. 42:5, 8). He is the eternal Creator, the great I Am. As the sovereign Ruler over heaven and earth, He separates the land and sea, the day and night, and He names all the stars. He can even rock the universe with one reverberating word from His mouth.

Yahweh can also meet the personal and spiritual needs of His worshipers. In contrast, could imitation gods bring us peace in the midst of our storms? Or protect us from danger? Or rescue us from trouble and turmoil? Could they inscribe our names on the palms of their hands out of deep love? Or provide us with eternal life in heaven?

Let's stand firm in our loyalties to Yahweh, enthroning Him as number one in our hearts. And let's make it a point to sit at His feet and get to know Him more deeply. Since *The God of All Truth* will win out in the end, let's joyfully proclaim—whether standing, kneeling, or falling on our faces—"The Lord, Yahweh, He is God!"

> Now when all the people saw [the Lord's
> consuming fire] they fell on their faces;
> and they said, "The Lord, He is God!"
> "The Lord [Yĕhovah], He is God!"
> (1 Kings 18:39)

WORSHIPPING GOD FOR HIS AWESOM-AZING ATTRIBUTES

He is omniscient, and He is/has immateriality and truthfulness.

Dear Lord, I worship You, The God of All Truth, who is gracious, loving, and all-knowing. Since You are pure Spirit, I will worship You in spirit and in truth. Please empower me to promote and defend

Your truth…to recognize and reject false teachings…to walk in love within the context of truth…and to fulfill my role of ministry in the battle for truth. For You are worthy of my service and my praise, and people's souls are incalculably valuable to You. In Jesus' name, amen.

OUR PRICELESS PATHWAY

Invites Us to Walk with Him

(Jesus declared:)
I am the way, the truth and the life. No one
comes to the Father except through Me.
(John 14:6)

Returning to the Shepherd's Path

"Give it up and get a divorce. You two are on *completely* different geometric planes, and you'll never connect," advised our fifth licensed marriage counselor. Though her remark communicated hopelessness, I made one more attempt to restore my ten-year marriage to Tom. I obtained the name of a Christian pastor to consult, but my husband was unwilling to go. Hurt and rejected, I finally filed for divorce and asked Tom to get out of my life.

I realized I was walking out of God's will, since I was the believing spouse in our unequally yoked marriage (see 1 Cor. 7:13). Yet I didn't think I could endure one more day feeling emotionally deserted.

We parted, and I didn't hear from Tom for eight months or so. Then one day my ex-husband left me an unexpected phone message. "Babe…Babe…I found Jesus in my life!"

Shocked, I replayed it. His voice had a passion I'd never heard. Humbled, I dropped to my knees. "God, I gave up on my husband, but You never did. Now he's a brother in Christ, bound for heaven. Thank You, Jesus!"

I rose to my feet, trying to process the new development. I knew a miracle had occurred, yet I still didn't want to reconcile. I feared falling back into the painful patterns we had experienced in our relationship.

When Tom phoned again, he invited me to meet him at a restaurant to share how he came to Christ. I was eager to hear about it. When I arrived, he was literally jumping for joy in the parking lot, shouting, "I've been liberated!" The man I had just divorced was definitely a new creation in Christ (2 Cor. 5:17).

After our conversation, Tom (who rarely gave gifts) presented me with a forest-green candle in a six-inch glass bowl lined with baby's breath. I could hardly believe it. But since I didn't want to indicate an interest in reconciling, I chose not to accept his gift. I'll never forget his sad face.

For months, the Holy Spirit continued to nudge me. Then one day, although I didn't hear an audible voice, the Lord spoke to my heart clearly and profoundly. "If you love Me, you will obey Me. And if you do, I will bless you and use you in a mighty way." I'd been going my own way, and I missed His fellowship. The Good Shepherd was calling me back onto His path (see John 14:15, 21).

Tom and I dated a few times. Finally, all my arguments against remarriage collapsed when he said, "If you were to marry me again, even if I lost everything I owned, I would still be a rich man because I would have you…and me…and the Lord."

Wow! What could I say but *yes*?

God has brought beauty out of the ashes of our marriage. Now my forest-green candle in the glass bowl lined with tiny lacy flowers, which decorates our guest room, is a reminder to me that Jesus Christ can connect *any* two spouses on *any* two geometric planes.

Is there an area in your life where God wants you to return to His path? In our times of personal failure, the Enemy of our souls tries to condemn us and draw us away from the Lord. But the Holy Spirit gently convinces us of our need to confess and draw closer than ever to the Lord, who loves us unconditionally (see Rom. 2:4; 8:1, 31–39).

If you enthrone Jesus in your heart, allowing Him to rule and reign in your life, you will enjoy an exciting intimacy with Him. You will also fulfill the individual plan of service God foreordained for you—bringing you the richest life possible because you'll be walking hand-in-hand with the Savior, *Our Priceless Pathway*.

> We are His workmanship [His poem, *poiēma* in Greek],
> created in Christ Jesus for good works, which God
> prepared beforehand that we should walk in them.
> (Eph. 2:10)

THE KING'S HIGHWAY TO HEAVEN

In the seventeenth century, John Bunyan penned his classical book *Pilgrim's Progress*.[134] In this allegory, the main character, named Christian, is set free from his burden of sins at the cross. At that moment, he becomes a child of God who enters the straight-and-narrow King's Highway leading to the Celestial City (heaven).

For the remainder of the book, Christian attempts to proceed on the pathway despite continual spiritual warfare—depicting the Christian life. He battles against the world, the flesh, and the devil. All three enemies tempt and derail him, using five "D ploys": deception, detour, discouragement, depression, and danger.

Behind the scenes, however, the sovereign Lord (*El Elyon* in Hebrew) protects, strengthens, matures, and delivers Christian. At the end of the story, he is welcomed into the Celestial City with trumpets and angels because he holds in his hand the required "passport of parchment." It symbolizes that he trusted in the finished work of Jesus Christ for his salvation and thus arrived on the only designated road.

In contrast, a character named Ignorance (whom Christian meets up with on two occasions) believes he will be allowed into heaven by his own good works instead of by God's free gift of grace. Even though Christian and his friend, Hopeful, try to persuade this fellow to get on the right road, he insists upon getting to heaven his way. Eventually, when Ignorance arrives at heaven's door and knocks, it won't open and he is cast into the horrible pit.

In true life, the King of kings has paved a road to heaven for us. We can enter heaven's gates only by coming through the costly sacrifice of Jesus Christ. When He declared, "It is finished!" the King's Highway opened up for transportation, with the grand offer of free admittance and free citizenship in heaven (John 19:30; Rom. 4:4–5). Tragically, however, those people who try to get to heaven on their own terms will meet with their doom.

Has God placed on your heart someone who is unenlightened about *Our Priceless Pathway*? If so, why not ask Him to prepare the soil of that person's heart and send a Spirit-led messenger to him or her. After all, parchment passports are invaluable, yet free of charge and freely available. And most important of all, they will never perish—nor will the new citizen.

> To him who works [tries to earn his way to heaven],
> the wages are not counted as grace but as debt. But to
> him who does not work but believes on Him who justifies
> the ungodly, his faith is accounted for righteousness.
> (Rom. 4:4–5)

A splash of living water and apologetics

THE UNIQUE GOD-MAN

The incarnation of Christ—God becoming man—is an essential doctrine of the Christian faith. Our Creator miraculously took on a body of flesh and dwelled among us on earth.[135] Jesus of Nazareth was fully God as well as fully man. (See Luke 22:66–71; John 1:1–3, 14; 5:18; 8:58; 14:11; 1 Tim. 3:16.)

Scriptures that teach the *deity of Christ* include Isaiah 9:6, John 8:24 and 58, John 17:5, and Revelation 1:8. By claiming the powerful title "I Am" (the personal name for God in Hebrew, seen in Exodus 3:14), Jesus indicated He was eternal and existing before Abraham lived.

Scriptures that teach the *humanity of Christ* include John 1:14 and Hebrews 2:14. In Philippians 2:7–8, we read that Jesus took the nature of a servant, being made in human likeness.

Only the sinless Lamb of God could qualify to be *Our Priceless Pathway* to heaven (John 1:29; 14:6). Glory be to God!

* * *

He [Jesus] needed to be divine to have the power
to *save* us, and He needed to be human in
order to adequately *represent* us.[136]
—Dr. Norman L. Geisler

MEETING LANDON ON THE AIRPLANE

"Here's your peanuts," I said to the teenager seated beside me on the airplane as I passed him the mini-snack. He sat upright, accepted the small bag with an engaging smile, and began a conversation. He wore an array of diamond studs in his earlobe, belly button, tongue, and nose. Landon turned out to be a personable high school junior from Oakland, newly elected as president of his class.

"I want you to know that my body piercing really isn't a sign of rebellion," he whispered.

I smiled, not sure what to say.

"You're probably wondering why I'm carrying around a teddy bear," he added, holding up a caramel-brown stuffed animal. "You see, I came from a wealthy family, but I didn't have much of a childhood. So I'm making up for lost time."

I knew God had arranged a divine appointment on my four-hour flight home to California. Yet I chuckled inwardly. *What topic could interest both a conservative older woman and a teenage guy emitting sparkles and clutching a teddy bear? What possible common ground could we have to talk about?*

As the hours and clouds flew by, Landon told me about himself and his family. I saw no opportunity to share about my Redeemer. When I realized the plane would be landing soon, I sent up a silent prayer.

Suddenly Landon shifted gears in his conversation. "I've been checking out various spiritual clubs on my campus," he said casually. "I visited the Satanic Club once, but now I'm more interested in joining the Buddhist group, I think. Some Christians invited me to the Bible Club a couple times, but I didn't go. I believe all roads lead to God."

I smoothly shifted into his gear. "At one time I believed all roads lead to God. It seemed like a courteous thing to do because then no one is wrong. But in my college Religions class, I found out that the various religions contradict each other in their main beliefs. So they can't possibly all lead to the same God."

"What do you mean?"

"Well, for example, some religions say there's only one God—that's called monotheism. And some say there are multiple gods—that's polytheism. Others say all things are God—that's pantheism. But logically, God can't be all of them. How could He be one God yet multiple gods at the same time? Or be a personal and impersonal God at the same time? So either all religions are wrong or only one of them is right."

Landon raised a couple more questions. I told him I was convinced that Jesus was the only road to heaven and that He rose from the dead to prove it. As the plane cruised down the landing strip, I told him that Jesus loved him and died for him.

When his turn came to exit the aircraft, he gave me a smile that seemed to emit more sparkles than his body jewelry. "Well, good-bye and good luck," he said, putting on his backpack. "Who knows, maybe I'll check out that Bible Club."

I may never see Landon again on this earth, but I pray that he *lands* in heaven someday. And I hope to see him there—with or without diamond studs and a teddy bear!

The next time you travel—whether on plane, train, boat, or bus—why not ask the Holy Spirit to seat you beside a truth seeker and inspire your words and thoughts? Then begin chatting. And don't be surprised if you hear yourself mention a life-changing Scripture, a salvation story, a nugget of apologetics, or the words *Jesus loves you.* If you do, eventually he or she might travel the proven highway—the one pointed out by the pierced hands of our Savior.

> You shall receive power when the Holy Spirit
> has come upon you; and you shall be witnesses
> to Me in Jerusalem, and in all Judea and

Samaria, and to the end of the earth [in your
city, your country, or internationally].
(Acts 1:8)

Devoted to the True Shepherd

Our Good Shepherd spoke these tender words concerning all of His disciples: "My sheep hear My voice, and I know them, and they follow Me" (John 10:27). He also said that His sheep would by no means follow a stranger, but would flee. For they associate only one voice with their genuine Shepherd, who cares for them and calls them by name (v. 3).

This principle is illustrated in the following true story, excerpted from a sermon by D. L. Moody. (It was originally told in the 1800s by Rev. Mr. Brown, referring to his friend in Syria.)[137]

> One day, as [my Syrian friend] was riding among the mountains, he came to a spring of water and stopped to rest awhile. Presently, down one of the steep mountain paths a shepherd came, leading his flock. Not long after, another shepherd with another flock came down to the water by another path, and after a while a third. The three flocks mingled together, so that my friend began to wonder how each shepherd was ever going to find his own sheep again.
>
> At last one of them rose up and called out, "*Men-ah!*" (which in Arabic means "Follow"), and his sheep came out from the great flock and followed him back into the mountains. He did not even stop to count them. Then shepherd No. 2 got up and called out to his sheep, "*Men-ah!*" And those of his flock left the others and followed him.
>
> My friend could speak Arabic very well, so one day he said to a shepherd, "I think I could make your sheep follow me."
>
> "I think not," said the shepherd.
>
> "Give me your turban and your cloak and your crook," said my friend, "and we'll see."

> So he put on the shepherd's turban and his cloak, and took the crook in his hand, and stood up where the sheep could see him, and called out, "*Men-ah! Men-ah!*" But not one sheep took any notice of him. They know not the voice of strangers.[138]

Our trustworthy Shepherd identified Himself as the world's Savior, who came to rescue all people who would believe in Him (John 3:16–21). He also said that those believers who would abide in (obey) His word would be His "disciples indeed" (John 8:31). And they would know the truth that sets people free (v. 32).

This grand offer stands true today. Let's be Jesus' *disciples indeed* by abiding in God's Word. If we do, we will recognize His voice more keenly, encounter Him more intimately, follow Him more consistently, and experience His freeing truth. Then we will naturally honor Him with our highest loyalty. For on the hill at Calvary, our Good Shepherd laid down His own life so that His beloved sheep could live forever.

> If you abide in My word, you are My disciples
> indeed. And you shall know the truth,
> and the truth shall make you free.
> (John 8:31–32)

FOCUSING OUR EYES ON JESUS

My first connection with William was when I overheard him shouting inside the Riverside County Jail. I could hear his voice in the background while I spoke to another inmate from a pay phone. Willy's passionate words impressed me: *I took my eyes off God, but I'm never taking my eyes off Him again!*

A few days later, I heard that Willy had formed a prayer chain among the inmates with the help of Miguel, another brother in the Lord. Every night several men held hands between the cell bars and prayed for their spouses, children, and personal needs.

If a guy didn't know how to pray, or didn't want to pray out loud, he would "pass" by squeezing the hand of the next guy in line to keep the prayers moving along. *Wow,* I thought. *God is really stirring men's hearts in there. And He has a mighty calling on Willy's and Miguel's lives.*

When I heard that Miguel drew a poignant picture depicting that nightly prayer chain, I wrote to him and asked if I could use it. His freehand drawing in pencil shows inmates on their knees, hand in hand, with their heads bowed in prayer. With his permission, that artwork now appears on the cover of a gospel tract titled "Why Pray to God?"[139]

Willy wrote the content of that pamphlet, which presents Jesus' pattern for prayer as seen in the Lord's Prayer (Matt. 6:9–13). The tract encourages readers to connect with God, through Jesus Christ, and develop a prayer life. By God's leading, that tract became the impetus for my prison tract ministry. To date, Miguel has created unique, lifelike art for nineteen tract covers, and Willy and Miguel have written powerful content for some of them.

During their time of incarceration, Willy and Miguel preached God's Word, led inmates to Christ, and took Bible college courses by correspondence. The Lord gave them both new beginnings in life, and they have introduced others to Him—often using their own tracts! I wouldn't be surprised if someday numerous ex-gang members and ex-convicts will arrive at heaven's gate, as new creations in Christ (holding out their "parchment passports").

God uses His children, wherever they are, to make known His gift of salvation. Do you know of Christian inmates or prison ministries you could pray for? Why not ask God to use them to share the glorious truth of Christ—as Paul the apostle asked the Colossian believers to do for him when he was imprisoned? If you do, surely more invaluable souls will connect to *Our Priceless Pathway* and then focus on a poignant picture of heaven, with living hope.

Meanwhile [pray] for us, that God would
open to us a door for the word, to speak
the mystery of Christ [the gospel],
for which I [Paul] am also in chains.
(Col. 4:3)

A splash of living water and apologetics

SIX BLIND MEN AND THE ELEPHANT

The following parable, which originated in India, is useful in defending Christianity's claim of exclusivity—that only one road leads to God (John 14:6).

Six blind men touch an elephant to learn what it's like. But each man feels a different part, so they all disagree. One blind man feels the leg and thinks the elephant is like a pillar; another feels the tail and thinks it's like a rope; another feels the trunk and thinks it's like a tree branch; another feels the tusk and thinks it's like a solid pipe.

A common misapplication of this parable is this: Since the six men described the same elephant quite differently, likewise all religions are describing a different aspect of the same God. Thus, all roads lead to God.

A more thoughtful and accurate application is this: All six blind men described the elephant incorrectly from their limited perspectives, yet the person telling the parable had the ability to see the entire elephant. His eyes were open to the big picture of truth. Thus, there is only one view of God that is fully truthful. And only one road leads to God.[140]

CRUMBLING COUNTERFEIT HIGHWAYS

My heart grieves for people who are unknowingly traveling on roads that lead to spiritual disaster. I'm tempted to roll down my car window and shout through a megaphone: *Hey, you're going the wrong way! There's a deadly hazard up ahead. Transfer to this road—the only reliable one—to reach your destination. It may look narrow, but it will accommodate any and all travelers.*

Hypothetically, if we were to warn vehicle drivers about impending danger, such as a collapsed highway up ahead, some of them would slam on their brakes and make a U-turn before reaching the roadway crisis. And they'd be ever grateful for the warning.

Likewise, we need to lovingly alert unbelievers about counterfeit religious highways that end at cliffs of destruction. Our loving Father desires that all precious souls on the *wide* road will place their faith in His Son so they can follow the *narrow* road that leads to life (Matt. 7:13–14).[141]

One reason that time is of the essence in sharing this good news is that people's life spans are unpredictable. Another reason is that Jesus Christ's second coming could be soon. The end-times Bible prophecies describing signs of the Lord's return are increasingly lining up with current events. Just one example is this: Matthew 24:7 alerts us to a time of increasing earthquakes around the world, and geophysicists have recorded more severe earthquakes in the last two decades than at any other period in history.[142]

Someday earth-quaking upheavals, provoked by shifting tectonic plates, will crumble the highways. Likewise, man's philosophies and religious systems—superficial roads to salvation—will collapse and fail. Only the God-given, enduring avenue will:

- lead us out of darkness into His marvelous light (1 Peter 2:9)

- lead us through royal gates made of solid pearl (Rev. 21:21)

- merge us onto the everlasting street of pure gold (Rev. 21:21)
- connect us face-to-face with the reigning King (Rev. 21:3–4).

Thank You, Abba Father, for Your immeasurable love for me, and for sending Your Son to be Our Priceless Pathway. I'm eternally grateful that Jesus is my Savior. That means I'm destined for the Celestial City…my hopes will never shatter…and my dreams will never crumble.

> Enter by the narrow gate; for wide is the gate and
> broad is the way that leads to destruction, and
> there are many who go in by it. Because narrow is
> the gate and difficult is the way which leads
> to life, and there are few who find it.
> (Matt. 7:13–14)

TUNING IN TO THE LORD'S VOICE

Picture a three-inch, shining-white angel on your right shoulder, whispering in your ear these heaven-sent words: "Do it this way and please God." Then on your left shoulder, picture a three-inch, pitchfork-carrying devil, blasting in your ear, "Do it this way and please yourself." Which will you choose to heed, God's still small voice or the persistent screams of the Enemy?

A retreat speaker I once heard used that vivid illustration to describe the Christian's ongoing spiritual battle, our inner conflict of spirit versus flesh.[143] All day long, we make moment-by-moment choices whether to yield to the Holy Spirit or yield to our flesh (see Gal. 5:16; Rom. 8:11–13).

In the book of Hebrews, we are exhorted to run our Christian race and stay on course consistently (Heb. 12:1). If we do, we will mature in faith, hold fast to truth, and grow in Christ-likeness. Every day is a significant lap in this race that's worth running to win (1 Cor. 9:24–25). We can stay on track and resist the selfish allurements that come our way by keeping our eyes fixed on Jesus, our inspiration (Heb. 12:2).

As we become more enamored with our Lord by encountering Him through prayer and Scripture, our sense of hearing will sharpen toward His voice. Those fickle-and-fleeting fleshly pleasures will lose their appeal. And when we start to stray to the left or right, our ears will discern His compassionate call, "Beloved, do not go that way." As Isaiah the prophet wrote, the Lord waits for our attention and longs for us to hear Him say, "This is the way, walk in it" (Isa. 30:21).

In the future, when we're in our glorified state, we will be able to hear Jesus speak to us audibly. When John the apostle was exiled on the island of Patmos, Jesus appeared in His heavenly glory and spoke to him distinctly (see Rev. 1:10–19).

Consider this dramatic scene for a moment. John is alone and exiled on this island, and suddenly he hears a loud voice behind him. When he turns around, he sees the Son of Man, whose countenance is like the bright shining sun and whose voice is magnified like a mighty waterfall. Overwhelmed, John falls down at Jesus' feet, but the Lord compassionately lays His right hand on the apostle and says, "Do not be afraid; I am the First and the Last" (v. 17). Then He asks John to record His revelations for seven churches.

While we wait for the privilege of engaging with Jesus face-to-face, we can regularly tune into our Savior's gentle whisper and reflect on His words, praying with a listening heart. By doing so, we will enjoy a two-way relationship with Him.

If you're not quite there yet, ask the Lord to help you hear His voice—through a gentle conviction, or a Scripture verse that comes to mind, or an inner peace, or a revelation in response to a prayer request. And dismiss the conflicting voices in your thought life by following the "3 Rs" based on James 4:7–8: *Recognize* the temptation at hand, *resist* the devil, and *rejoice* in the Lord as you draw near to Him and submit. Then you will experience a rich and meaningful journey through life with *Our Priceless Pathway*, whose loving voice you will always treasure.

> Your ears shall hear a word behind you,
> saying, "This is the way, walk in it,"
> whenever you turn to the right hand
> or whenever you turn to the left.
> (Isa. 30:21)

SHOUTING, "SHIP AHOY!"

My beloved husband and I typically talk apples and oranges together. We are opposites in most everything, beginning with personality. For example, Tom has an engineer's mind-set and loves to major in life's basics. He speaks primarily the language of Mechanical-eze, and he doodles in black-and-white geometric boxes. (Don't you agree that doodling styles can reveal volumes about people?) In contrast, I have a writer's mind-set and love to consider endless possibilities in life's issues. I speak primarily the language of Christian-eze, and I doodle in colorful flowers and hearts.

Recently we had a real "connecting conversation" when Tom walked in the front door after his early-morning trip to the gym. During my trip through devotions at the kitchen table, I had come up with an idea about his recent retirement from his career as a corporate executive.

"Pooky," I blurted out as he entered the front door. (Please don't tell anyone I called my husband Pooky!) "I just had a wonderful breakthrough during my prayer time, and I want to tell you about it. I'll need your undivided attention for five or six minutes, okay?"

He pulled up a chair and sat down, threw his workout towel over his shoulder, then requested my bottom line.

"Throughout our marriage, you've worked very hard for various companies as the general manager and director of engineering. You've provided well for our family and steered a smooth-running ship. Meanwhile, I've worked hard as a mom, student, and employee—and more recently as a writer of Christian tracts. Well, I believe the Captain of our ship is calling us both into the tract ministry. Together we can make an even greater difference for Christ!"

I practically stood on my chair with excitement. My husband just rolled his eyes. But I was determined to help him catch my vision.

"You could use your organizational skills and your make-it-happen abilities to expand the broadcasting system for True-Way Tracts. You could also discover how to get more traffic to our website so many more boats could come in off the main channels and wander into our inlet."

Tom raised an eyebrow at my stretched metaphor. His body even rocked from side to side, as if he were getting a little seasick.

Ignoring his skepticism, I continued. "I feel like I'm wearing myself out by using Morse Code to communicate God's mega-message to ships at sea. Relatively few have received my SOS warning that there's only one safe landing up ahead. All ships are on the home stretch, with only twenty-five knots to go."

"Not knots," Tom corrected. "That's a unit of speed. You mean nautical miles."

"And you could be a navigator directing them to the Lighthouse of eternal safety." With waving arms, I spit out my grand finale. "Wouldn't that be great if ships heeded our Captain's call and shifted their course before they became *Titanics*?"

Tom stood up. "I'll look into it." He sauntered down the hallway toward his office. Yet I was sure I detected a smile on his face. I interpreted his vague comment to mean, "Go ahead and toss out that Morse Code machine; it's time to shout, 'Ship ahoy' in cyberspace!" Okay, maybe I was just hearing what I wanted to hear.

As it turned out, Tom did join me in the TWT ministry by co-hosting our resource booth at evangelistic conferences. And step by step, God is opening distribution channels for our materials in cyberspace and elsewhere. Thankfully, my husband and I pray for God's will in our lives. And we worship *Our Priceless Pathway*, who always knows what's around the next bend and leads us according to what's best for us.

Do you pray for God to unfold His ministry plan for you so that you can fit into it? Or do you pray for God to bless your plan of ministry and join you in it? There's a big difference. God's personalized plan for you was set forth long ago (Eph. 2:10). The Holy Spirit will be your divine Navigator, and His path will lead to abundant spiritual fruit. So keep praying for God to show you His will, step by step or knot by knot.

> It is God who works in you both to will
> and to do for His good pleasure.
> [He gives you the desire to obey Him
> and the power to do what pleases Him].
> (Phil. 2:13)

A splash of living water and apologetics

ONLY ONE ROAD REACHES HEAVEN?

Christianity is the most humble religion there is, as it's the only one that acknowledges that no one is good enough to get into heaven on his own.[144] Nobody can earn his way into the presence of holy God. The only thing people can do is decide to receive God's free gift of salvation (Eph. 2:8–9).[145]

In fact, since unbelievers are lost and dying and have no Savior, the most loving and important message anyone could ever share with them is the biblical teaching that only one road reaches heaven. And all who trust in Jesus for their salvation will freely enter that glorious road.

> *Our Priceless Pathway*, Jesus Christ, demonstrated His profound love for us at the cross of Calvary. There He bore the penalty for everyone's sins (John 1:29) so they could be forgiven. Then He declared that whoever believes in Him will be reborn and destined for heaven (John 3:3, 16).
>
> Now, that's God's grace, which brings us to our knees in gratitude and adoration!
>
> * * *
>
> *Jesus told us:*
> *"Greater love has no one than this, than*
> *to lay down one's life for his friends."*
> *(John 15:13)*

WALKING WITH OUR GOOD SHEPHERD

When did you first realize you had a Good Shepherd watching over you? Was it immediately upon receiving Christ? For me, it was when I was a kid, kneeling beside my bed with clasped hands, reciting my nightly bedtime prayer: "Our Father, who art in heaven, hallowed be Thy name…Give us this day our daily bread…and deliver us from evil." (I didn't know at the time that this wording came from the model prayer that Jesus gave us in Matthew 6.)

Our Priceless Pathway not only provides us safe passage to heaven, He journeys with us through life, desiring to share a beloved sheep-and-shepherd relationship with us. King David, who once was a dedicated shepherd himself, portrays our Lord in the Twenty-Third Psalm in three marvelous capacities:[146]

- *Our loving Shepherd (Psalm 23:1–3a)*

As His cherished sheep, we shall not lack anything necessary or beneficial for us, day by day. With tender affection, our Shepherd provides times for us to lie down and rest in green pastures, and He leads us beside peaceful waters, and restores our souls.

Since our loving and all-wise Shepherd is working all things together for our good, if we don't receive something we've asked Him for in prayer, we can be assured that it's not good for us, or not the best for us, or the timing isn't right (Rom. 8:28).

- *Our caring Guide (Psalm 23:3b–4)*

Our Guide leads us in the paths of righteousness, bringing honor to His name. He directs us by His Word, by His providence, and by our conscience.[147] He walks close beside us and comforts and protects us with His rod and staff. So we need not fear.

If we will trust our divine Guide with all our hearts and acknowledge Him in all our ways (instead of depending on our own understanding), He will keep us safe and direct our paths toward what is good and true and right (see Prov. 3:5–7).

- *Our gracious Host (Psalm 23:5–6)*

Even in the presence of our enemies, our gracious Host prepares a banquet to sustain us. He anoints our heads with the oil of gladness and fills our cups to overflowing with blessings and provisions. His goodness and mercy pursue us daily.

Since our Shepherd-Host holds the Enemy at bay, we can enjoy loving fellowship with Him in peace and security. We can also fulfill our individual callings in life and anticipate dwelling with Him forever (John 14:2). Hallelujah!

Dear Lord, thank You for Your faithfulness as my loving Shepherd, caring Guide, and gracious Host. Thank You for paying the price for me to join Your flock, for loving me and guiding me, and for providing for all my needs. I will walk near You and trust in You. Covered with your oil of gladness right now, I want to proclaim to others that…

The Lord is my shepherd; I shall not want
[He provides everything I need].
(Ps. 23:1)

SPIRITUAL GLIMMERS ON A ROAD WITHOUT PROMISE

During my "BC" days (*before* meeting Christ), I traveled through life on a road without hope. I didn't realize that I lacked the assurance of heaven or that I lived without full dimension or true joy. I perceived only glimmers of spiritual truth as I functioned in the natural realm (see 1 Cor. 2:14). Thankfully, God had brought some Scripture into my heart in my early years when my father preached and the congregation sang hymns. And Isaiah 55:11 promises that His word will prosper wherever He sends it.

One Easter Sunday, when my twin sister and I were age eleven, we sang in the church choir. When the organ began to play, we stood up without a hymnal and cheerfully boomed our voices over the balcony banister. "Christ the Lord is risen today. A-a-a-a-a-lelujah. Raise your joys and triumphs high. A-a-a-a-a-lelujah!"[148]

When some of the congregants below us turned to look our way, Carolyn and I suddenly realized that the choir had moved on to the first verse and we only knew the opening stanza. We quickly ducked down and tried to fade into the pew! I'll never forget that embarrassing incident from childhood, but the hymn did instill in my heart and mind the extraordinary news that our Lord rose from the dead. In fact, recalling Jesus' resurrection still sometimes leads me to sing "A-a-a-a-a-lelujah!"

My twin sister and I enjoyed a close relationship as kids. At times we even communicated without words, since we knew each other so well as companions and confidants. Occasionally, we even spoke a secret language our cousin taught us, based on a phonetic formula. Our "Twin-Latin" came in handy, especially when we wanted to share jokes without being overheard.

Now, in my "AC" days (*after* meeting Christ), I enjoy intimate communication with my Savior, who knows my words and thoughts even before I think them (Ps. 139:1–4). I can take everything to Him in prayer, knowing that He fully understands me, loves me, and forgives me. And I travel the road of promise, which carries assurances of heaven, purpose, joy, and more. In fact right now, I'm bending over a balcony banister and belting out praises to *Our Priceless Pathway,* who gave me life!

Do you know a churchgoer who recites Bible verses and sings worship songs but is trying to get into heaven (or mature spiritually) by doing enough good works? I once fell into the trap of legalism, attempting to earn God's favor by following rules and regulations. Although it's our human tendency to think that way, God's astounding gospel is that we're saved entirely by His grace, through faith in Christ (Eph. 2:8–9; see also John 1:17; Col. 2:20–23).

Why not share your salvation story with a church attender who's burdened by legalism? Just think. Someday that person might respond to God's grace as a free gift—and then go on to enjoy a new beginning and a new family, as well as new values, motivations, and possessions.[149] If so, that new believer could enjoy blessed communication with the One who perfectly understands His children. And who knows? He or she might even lean over some roof or railing and shout, "A-a-a-a-a-lelujah!"

> If anyone is in Christ, he is a new creation
> [with the Holy Spirit dwelling within];
> old things have passed away; behold,
> all things have become new.
> (2 Cor. 5:17)

WORSHIPPING GOD FOR HIS AWESOM-AZING ATTRIBUTES

He is jealous, and He is/has moral perfection.

Lord, thank You for being Our Priceless Pathway, who paved the way for me to reach the Celestial City someday and who walks with me every day. I worship You for Your character, which is holy, loving, and morally perfect. Thank You for loving me with a godly jealousy, desiring my love from an undivided heart. For You are a jealous God, who has a zeal for preserving Your nature, Your name, Your people, Your land, and Your city.[150] I love You and I devote myself to You fully. In Jesus' name, amen.

THE EVERLASTING GOD

OFFERS US ETERNAL LIFE WITH HIM

Have you not known? Have you not heard?
The everlasting God, the Lord, the Creator of the
ends of the earth, neither faints nor is weary.
His understanding is unsearchable.
(Isa. 40:28)

A BEE STING IN THE CHEMISTRY LAB

SHORTLY BEFORE NOON, I darted through the corridors of Richmond High, searching for the chemistry lab. As guest speaker for the Bible Club, which met weekly during the school's lunch hour, I didn't want to be late. Security guards lined the hallways and several teenage girls carried babies in and out of a nursery classroom. Times had certainly changed since I'd stepped onto a high school campus!

When I entered the chemistry lab, I introduced myself to the club sponsor. While setting up my notes, I glanced at the room full of students. To my surprise, many of their faces bore tattoos. But the symbols emblazoned on their skin were crosses and crowns of thorns. These teenagers were standing up for Christ, even in the hostile environment of high school.

While I spoke on the topic of "How Can a God of Love Allow Pain and Suffering?" I encountered something else I hadn't expected. Just as I reached the last page of my presentation notes, a bumble bee stung me on the palm of my hand.

I didn't know whether to laugh or cry. Since the windows along one wall of the laboratory were cranked wide open to welcome sunshine and warmth, it wasn't surprising that the culprit had gotten in. But I'm allergic to bee stings! Could the Enemy be trying to sabotage my mission? If that was spiritual warfare, I thought, it wasn't going to discourage me from coming back two more Wednesdays to finish my apologetics lecture series.

After I removed the stinger from my hand, the chemistry teacher immediately concocted an ointment there in the lab, and then applied it to my wound to extract any remaining poison.

The students remained speechless—a bit shocked, I suspected. Why else would a bunch of teenagers not be laughing at this? When I looked up, I saw them all staring at me with frozen faces, and motionless hands clutching sandwiches. Finally one girl explained.

Apparently, as I was discussing the concept of eternity and making a figure eight in the air with my arms to illustrate the infinity symbol, one of my hands landed on the bee, which instinctively retaliated. At that moment, I was trying to make the point that God sometimes allows temporary pain for good eternal purposes. (I wonder if any of the students thought I had planned for a bee to sting me to emphasize my point!)

As I indicated in my lecture, God is not to blame for human misery, as Satan would have us believe. Sin, death, and evil entered the world when men and angels rebelled against Him. As a result, we are now fallen people living in a fallen world (see Gen. 3; Isa. 14:12–15).

Our ability to understand *Our Everlasting God,* and His power, is vastly limited (Isa. 40:28). But we do know that He loves all people and desires us to receive salvation and not perish

(2 Peter 3:9). So sometimes He uses hardships to get the attention of unbelievers so they will consider such eternal matters.

As for believers, although we can't know all of the reasons God allows suffering in our lives, Scripture tells us that there is purpose in it. He will sustain us and carry us through it, and when all our afflictions are over, our joys will never end (2 Cor. 4:17–18).

It didn't take long for the palm of my hand to heal after that bee sting. Today, I can even laugh about the incident. And in retrospect, if given the choice, I would experience the whole thing again if necessary for the opportunity to speak to teens about defending the Christian faith.

When we live to glorify God, sacrifices are occasionally required. Yet because He sacrificed so greatly to redeem us—out of His infinite love for us—we are motivated to love, serve, and testify of Him (yet not necessarily by tattooing our faces with crosses!). Someday, when God wipes away all our tears and there's no more sorrow or pain, surely we will acknowledge that our troubles on earth were worth it all. For any temporary stings in our present life are infinitesimally brief compared to our eternity, with only heavenly bliss (Rev. 21:3–7).

> What is the nature of your life? You are [really] but a
> wisp of vapor—a puff of smoke, a mist—that is visible
> for a little while and then disappears [into thin air].
> (James 4:14 AMP)

A BRIDEGROOM'S FOREVERMORE LOVE SONG

Have you ever attended a wedding that was remarkably romantic? When my son got married several years ago, he surprised his beautiful bride—and all the guests—by adding a unique flair to the ceremony. In advance of the big day, Tony wrote a wedding song with his own guitar accompaniment, expressing his forever-more love to Linda.

Right after the bride and groom recited their vows at the altar, Tony got down on one knee in his black tux, positioned his guitar and shoulder strap, then tenderly sang his musical composition called "Precious Love." I'm sure many hearts melted besides Linda's.

After the minister pronounced them man and wife, the brawny groom (at six feet tall and two hundred pounds) passionately kissed his petite bride (at five feet tall and ninety-eight pounds), then scooped her up into his arms. With Linda's lacy veil and white satin train flowing behind, Tony carried her down the aisle to the front door of the church. As my heart skipped to the wedding march, I heard sighs and sniffles all around me.

Over the years, Tony and Linda have continued their devotion to each other. They are raising three children who love to hear me tell the story of their parents' romantic wedding in which their dad sang his touching song and carried their mom down the aisle, in charming Hollywood style.

Here are some of the lyrics Tony sang, which echo the words of our Bridegroom to us:

> There are no words I can use to describe how I love you.
> We could be one, no longer two.
> I'll hold you close to me; I'll never let you go.
> Let's shine together, our lives forever.
> I love you. Be one with me.[151]

Our Everlasting God loves us with a never-ending, never-changing love. Jesus told us about this divine love: "For God so loved [*agapaō*] the world that He gave [sacrificed] His only begotten Son, that whoever believes in Him should not perish but have everlasting life" (John 3:16).

Someday our Bridegroom will surprise us by His glorious presence…and lift us into His arms…and express His love to us face-to-face. As the saying goes, it will be a marriage made in heaven.

All believers are given the title "bride of Christ." The New Testament refers to Jesus as the Bridegroom and His church as His bride. The Old Testament refers to the nation of Israel as the bride of Yahweh.

Does your cherished title of "Jesus' bride" remind you that you will enjoy a never-ending relationship with the Lover of your soul, who laid down His life for you? In response to His deep personal love for you, do you keep Him on the throne of your heart? After all, He rejoices over you with singing (Zeph. 3:17) and will remain devoted to you forevermore.

(God declares to us:)
Yes, I have loved you with an everlasting love;
therefore with lovingkindness I have drawn you.
(Jer. 31:3)

DIVINE DELAYS ARRANGED IN HEAVEN

When Abraham finally acted on his divine call from God, he was seventy-five years old and his wife, Sarah, was sixty-five. God instructed Abraham to follow His leading to another land, away from his home country (with its pagan religions) and far from all his kin. God promised to make him the father of a great nation, to bless him personally, and to bless all the families of the earth through him. (For the Messiah would arise out of Abraham's lineage and provide salvation for the world!) (See Gen. 12:1–3.)

Sarah got on board with God's calling, even knowing that hardship would follow them as they headed to parts unknown. Yet she wondered how she'd have children, since she was barren.

The couple remained childless for years. But one day God graciously renewed His promise to Abraham that he'd father a son who would be his heir (Gen. 15:4). Not understanding this divine delay, Sarah decided to help God out by devising a carnal plan: her husband could sleep with her maidservant, Hagar, so she'd bear children for Sarah. Although Hagar did conceive and have a child (16:16), Ishmael was not the son of promise.

It was not until Abraham reached one hundred, and Sarah ninety (well past the age of childbearing), that Sarah miraculously bore Isaac. Sure enough, after they waited twenty-five years, God fulfilled His promise to them regarding the promised son. Both of them passed their tests of faith and appear in the Hebrews "Hall of Faith" (Heb. 11:8–12, 17–19). God's plan of redemption for mankind was unfolding. One day our Redeemer would arrive through the Jewish nation.

Sometimes it seems like God is dragging His feet in fulfilling His promises because our circumstances aren't changing as quickly as we'd like. Yet God's timetable is never one day or even one hour too soon or too late. (See Isa. 46:9–11; 48:3–5; Rev. 1:8, 11.) As one Bible expositor writes: "Our lives are not given over to blind fate, to random meaninglessness, or to endless cycles with no resolution. Instead, Jesus Christ, who is the Alpha and the Omega, the Beginning and the End, directs all of human history and even our individual lives."[152]

Do you trust the Lord in situations when His timing is different from yours? Instead of losing heart or trying to hurry God along, wait on Him patiently and you will pass the test of faith. Since He is the everlasting King (*El Olam*[153]; see Jer. 10:10), you can be sure that His plan is flawless. His Word is infallible. His power is unlimited. His love is unfailing. He is infinitely trustworthy. And His timing is perfect.

> Trust in the Lord forever,
> for in YAH [Yahweh], the Lord,
> is everlasting strength.
> (Isa. 26:4)

A splash of living water and apologetics

AMAZING FULFILLED BIBLE PROPHECY

Our Everlasting God, who lives outside of time, is the only one capable of foretelling future events—literally, precisely, and extensively. Through Scripture, He has revealed to us history in advance.

Bible prophecy, and its amazing fulfillment, establishes that the Bible is a unified message from our Creator. Consider this staggering evidence:

- its extensiveness (one thousand predictive prophecies, comprising about one-fourth of the Bible[154])

- its fulfillment with 100 percent accuracy (five hundred prophecies fulfilled literally to date[155])

- its preciseness (with details and specifics)

- its accurate correlation with history

- its complete harmony throughout Scripture

- its consistent focus on Messiah (the Christ) and His mission to redeem the human race.

In contrast, all other books regarded as religious Scripture fall hopelessly short. They contain little if any prophecy, and none dares to claim any significant historical fulfillment.[156]

(See an apologetics brief on this subject, referenced in the endnote.[157])

MEETING MY FAVORITE BIBLE TEACHER

Several years ago I flew to Chattanooga, Tennessee, to attend a week of inductive Bible study training held on the campus of Precept Ministries International. I was excited about becoming a trained Precept Bible study leader. I also looked forward to personally meeting Kay Arthur—the ministry's founder, popular author, and Bible teacher.

Toward the end of the week, however, I learned that Kay was traveling and not available. The only chance I had to meet her was at the airport, since she'd be flying in about the same time I'd be flying out.

A special window of opportunity opened at the airport terminal. To my utter amazement, I ended up sitting right next to Kay's husband, Jack Arthur, and her sweet mother. They had invited me to sit with them. As all three of us waited to greet the same person about to step off the plane, Jack talked about possibly writing a book on his missionary adventures in Africa, and Kay's mom and I spoke about our similar church backgrounds.

When Kay exited the plane, I witnessed a precious homecoming. She headed straight for Jack with starry eyes and a glowing smile. Then she leaned forward and tenderly stroked his cheeks as if to say, "I missed you so very much!" The Bible teacher I admired was demonstrating in real life one of the biblical roles of a wife—to express love and admiration to her spouse.

After Kay greeted her mom, I introduced myself. During our delightful five-minute conversation, she asked my opinions about the Precept training week and the trainers. After giving favorable feedback, I waved good-bye and headed for my own plane.

I couldn't wait to get home to greet my husband, Tom, just like my role model had done. I exited the plane with starry eyes and a glowing smile. Then I approached him and tenderly stroked his cheeks. But to my surprise, Tom reacted much differently than

Jack. With a frown on his face, he said, "What's the matter, didn't I shave this morning?" We both laughed.

Many blessings resulted from my week of training in Chattanooga, where I gained skills in "rightly dividing the Word of God" (2 Tim. 2:15). Although I never did lead a Precepts study, I hosted several sessions of Kay's Bible study *Lord, Heal My Hurts* in my home. My love for God's Word continued to grow. And two years later, Kay graciously took the time to review and endorse my first three apologetics tracts, which launched my Christian tract ministry. The God of the Big Picture graciously networks people, places, and things together.

Now, whenever I return home from traveling, I make it a point to greet Tom lovingly (regardless of whether he shaved that morning!). For when I minister to him, I am also ministering to our Lord (Eph. 5:22). That principle became unforgettable to me after my firsthand observation of the founder of Precept Ministries at the Chattanooga airport.

Do you marvel at how *Our Everlasting God* directs your path when you fully trust in Him and don't depend on your own understanding? Proverbs 3:5–6 instructs us to do that, meaning we'd be wise to follow His leading because His ways are far better than ours.

From now on, when you lift up your personal petitions to Abba Father, why not conclude by saying, "Even so, may *Your* will be done." By welcoming Him to override your desires, you display great faith in Him. Sometimes He'll answer your prayers in ways that surprise you and bless you beyond your expectations. And over time, when you look back at how He guided your path, you might even see the eternal wisdom behind it.

(Moses prayed:)
Before the mountains were brought forth,
[before You] formed the earth and the world,
even from everlasting to everlasting, You are God.
(Ps. 90:2)

GOD IS WORKING BEHIND THE SCENES

My papa's health crisis tugged at my heart strings and tied my stomach into knots. A huge decision needed to be made regarding his developing dementia.

After my step-mom graduated into heaven, Papa's health steadily declined. At first, he moved into an assisted-care facility near his friends, made a few new ones, and enjoyed presenting paperback Bibles at his hospital calls—continuing to minister to others.

Two years later, he transferred into an immediate-care facility. One day the administrator notified me that Papa's escalating dementia caused him to have "swatting episodes." Since the facility couldn't risk having injuries to other residents, he recommended that Papa be placed in a facility with locked doors. He had thirty days to leave.

Lord, I can't put my beloved Papa in a locked facility. There's got to be another option! Please open another door for him. For three weeks, I searched for an appropriate facility. But no resolution presented itself.

With one week left, the phone rang. A woman named Bettie said she had met "Father John" (my papa) a few years earlier. The two of them had a mutual friend, Marian, who resided at the same assisted-living place where Papa previously lived.

"Marilyn," she said, "I just acquired my nursing certification and a permit to care for patients in my home. I have four available bedrooms, and I'd love for Marian and your papa to be my first two resident-patients."

Marveling at the offer, yet wanting to be completely honest, I responded, "Bettie, I'd love to meet you and discuss that possibility. But you'll probably reconsider when I tell you about my papa's spontaneous hand-swatting."

"Oh, I've worked in the nursing field for a long time," she said without hesitation. "I can assure you that I've never encountered a dementia patient I couldn't handle."

With misty eyes, I blurted out, "Well, you might just be an angel in disguise!"

Papa went to live in Bettie's care facility, and she treated him like a member of her own family. He especially enjoyed her two grandchildren, who often climbed up on his lap in his wheelchair, wrapped their arms around him with big hugs, and called him Father John.

And do you know what? Papa never had another swatting episode. The loving atmosphere in Bettie's small nursing home overcame his illness-related fears. And I do believe Bettie was an angel whom *Our Everlasting God* sent to minister His love to Papa.

God knew. God heard.

God answered. And God loved.

Thank You, Abba Father, for dispensing boundless grace when I call on You in times of desperation for my own needs or when I intercede for others. I'm amazed at how You work behind the scenes when we petition heaven, and how You demonstrate Your infinite love, which casts out fear—sometimes through people or angels.

> There is no fear in love; but [knowing
> God's] perfect love casts out fear.
> (1 John 4:18)

"Behold Your God!"

Embedded in the messianic portion of the book of Isaiah is a magnificent sketch of the coming Messiah—previewing a deep and utterly amazing coming attraction.

In Isaiah 40, God instructs His prophet to comfort and encourage His people, in Jerusalem, by letting them know they no longer needed to feel burdened. Their sins had been completely paid for (after seventy years' of judgment) (vv. 1–2), and now He wants to give them blessings.[158] For He is back in their lives.

In verses 3–11, an unidentified voice "crying in the wilderness" heralds good news of the coming Christ. Isaiah speaks up for this personal forerunner to the King, declaring to the people this (summarized) message:

> Prepare the way for the coming King of glory. Make "the crooked places" straight by preparing your hearts (vv. 3–4). The glory of the Lord will be revealed to all mankind[159] (v. 5). In contrast to people's lives, which wither and fade, the powerful Word of God will stand forever. So the Lord will fulfill all of His promises (vv. 6–8). These good tidings need to be shouted out. So get up to the high mountain and proclaim to the cities of Judah, "Behold your God!" (v. 9). The Messiah will come as a ruling king and bring His reward. He will also come as a loving shepherd, intending to deliver[160] His flock and faithfully care for them (vv. 10–11).

Isaiah also comforts the people by declaring God's outstanding character. Beholding His attributes would usher them into praise and adoration. He is the author of creation (v. 12), omniscient (vv. 13–14), sovereign (vv. 15–17), incomparable (vv. 18–21), omnipotent (vv. 22–24), sustainer (vv. 25–26), eternal (vv. 27–28), compassionate (vv. 29–30), and trustworthy (v. 31).

Meditating on these attributes of God has the same effect on us today, escorting us into awe and worship. As you gaze upon *Our Everlasting God*, are you astonished that He desires to relate to you personally? Are you blessed beyond belief that you know, serve, and adore the prophesied Messiah?

Although you might not climb up a mountain to declare the good tidings, you could use your spiritual giftings to advance the gospel. For example, you might encourage, support, or pray for God's missionaries. Then needy souls—who hear and receive salvation—will not *wither and fade*, but will remain secure in God's everlasting grip.

The eternal God is your refuge, and
underneath are [His] everlasting arms.
(Deut. 33:27)

A splash of living water and apologetics

GOD'S PURPOSE FOR PROPHECY

"The Bible itself declares fulfilled prophecy to be the built-in proof of its divine origin."[161] In the book of Isaiah, God announced why He gave hundreds of predictive prophecies to mankind: He revealed specific events before they happened so that when they came to pass, it would show that He is the only true and living God. (See Isa. 42:8–9; 44:7–8; 46:9–11; 48:3–6.)[162]

God has accomplished (and is still accomplishing) His stated purpose. He declared; He fulfills! Thus, predictive prophecy and its fulfillment confirm that the Bible is authentic and Jehovah is God.

As prophecy scholar John F. Walvoord points out, "Unmistakably, the evidence is overwhelming that God means exactly what He says, as prophecy after prophecy has already been literally fulfilled. When history has run its course, every prophecy will be fulfilled."[163]

* * *

I am God, and there is none like Me,
declaring the end from the beginning...
Indeed I have spoken it; I will also bring it
to pass. I have purposed it; I will also do it.
(Isa. 46:9–11)

PENGUINS AND PADDLES

Hanging on the wall next to my computer is a watercolor painting of a party of penguins enjoying the snow in Alaska. It's there to remind me of a mental image I had of myself acting like a proud penguin, standing on an iceberg with paddle in hand. The iceberg represented the Christian ministry I longed to advance. Foolishly and furiously, I tried to move the massive mound of floating ice by my own paddling efforts.

Do you know how much icebergs weigh? I recently received an e-mail picturing a giant iceberg in Newfoundland, with an estimated weight of 300,000,000 tons. And remember, just one iceberg sank the allegedly indestructible *Titanic*. Yet I naively thought I could move one with my own good intentions and hard work.

When I realized the futility of my efforts, I surrendered my paddle to the Lord and asked Him to take over steering the iceberg (as well as to thaw out my frozen blockhead!). If *Our Everlasting God* can direct the ocean currents, surely He is capable of guiding the paths of our lives. He decides when to move an "iceberg"—whether it represents a ministry, or a personal breakthrough, or a person's salvation. And He sees beneath the tip of the iceberg, knowing what He aims to accomplish and how.

Back then, I was trying to fight for God's kingdom (which is a spiritual battle) in my own abilities—kind of like Peter did when he tried to defend Jesus in the garden of Gethsemane. He drew his sword and struck the servant of the high priest, cutting off his ear. But Jesus replaced and healed Malchus's ear because Peter's action did not line up with God's mighty plan (see Luke 22:51; John 18:10–11).

We can actually get in God's way by trying to make ministry happen, for it's the Holy Spirit who accomplishes God's work, using us as His instruments. That was the message given to Zerubbabel. He had led a group of people back to their Jewish homeland, and his responsibility was to finish up the work of rebuilding the temple. The Lord's encouraging word to him was "'Not by might nor by power, but by My Spirit,' says the Lord of hosts" (Zech. 4:6). Or, as one commentator translates that verse, "It is not by [your] brawn or by [your] brain, but by my Spirit" that the temple would be rebuilt.[164]

Do you gladly serve our worthy God yet sometimes get weary because the task you face is much bigger than you are? Why not turn over your rowing oars to the Holy Spirit in prayer, trusting Him to lead you. Instead of striving or going ahead of Him, wait on Him with expectancy. At the right time, He will strengthen you and work through you. Then *Our Everlasting God*—who "neither faints nor is weary" (Isa. 40:28)—will finish the work, and all the glory will go to Him.

> Those who wait on the Lord shall renew their
> strength; they shall mount up with wings like
> eagles, they shall run and not be weary,
> they shall walk and not faint.
> (Isa. 40:31)

RUPERT'S BLOG POST GLORIFYING GOD

Although my friend Rupert still lives in the homeless shelter and hasn't yet reached the elusive Viability Road (as of the date of this writing, anyway), I have high hopes for him. For he continues to pray for God's will to be done in his life, and he glorifies *Our Everlasting God* through his writings.

After Rupert's season of sidewalk living (which lasted ninety-eight days), he wrote the following blog post, in which he presented a heartfelt testimony about Jesus' presence in his life at that time:

> Things are not what they were 90, 60, or even 30 days ago. They are better. The name of this blog is Rupert Loves Jesus. I rarely talk about my personal experience with Him

because it feels like I'm turning this into a platform in which to preach about religion. I don't do religion. We might get into a discussion about denominations, but religion is something I try to stay away from. I just talk about what I know, and I know I prayed my biscuits off!

I'm not really a testimonial type of guy, so I'll keep this brief. It was Jesus Christ who protected me in times of imminent harm and complete horror. Jesus listened when I had no one to talk to, and He heard all my appeals. I am blessed in the areas that matter, and the other stuff is handled by Him anyhow.

I'm not a theological expert, and I can't preach for much, but my God is personal, and things are pretty real for me, and that is not always good, but sometimes it is necessary.

Every believer is in ministry. Rupert calls it "representing" Jesus in our journeys. My friend continues to represent the Lord through his so-called "squiblet" writings and short stories. Recently, he even wrote a testimony tract for homeless people about God's faithfulness, titled "Where is God…and Why Won't He Help Me?"[165]

Each of us has opportunities to shine our light by sharing our experiences with Jesus. Personal testimonies are "miraculous examples of God's grace and love, and of the Holy Spirit's power to transform lives."[166] They are powerful witnesses because they are "personal" and "pretty real," and thus cannot be denied.

Why not record how God has faithfully intervened in your life and how He answered your prayers in His way and in His timing? Then you can "represent" and glorify our worthy God by relating those incidents to others. After all, it was out of deep compassion for us that He inscribed our names on the palm of His hand (Isa. 49:16). The hands of *Our Everlasting God* were literally pierced on the cross—for you, me, and everyone—to say, *I love you.*

(Paul testified:)
Suddenly a great light from heaven shone around
me [Saul]. And I fell to the ground and heard a voice
saying to me, "Saul, Saul, why are you persecuting
Me?" So I answered, "Who are You, Lord?" And
He said to me, "I am Jesus of Nazareth."
(Acts. 22:6–8)

HIS WONDROUS WAYS TOWARD US

Dear Christian brother or sister, I hope that as you've gone through these devotions that showcase our awesom-azing God, you've marveled at His attributes, engaged with Him in sweet fellowship, and proclaimed Him to others. I trust that you have basked in His unconditional love and have allowed Him to quench your spiritual thirst. As missionary Elizabeth Elliott wrote, "I was made for God, [so] my heart will never rest anywhere else, and nothing the world can offer will satisfy."[167]

Why not spend some time right now capturing some of the wondrous ways God has personally related to you? Listed below are the subtitles of our ten chapters. On a separate tablet or on your computer, record a praise report, or a biblical lesson learned, or a prayer of thanksgiving, or an experience related to each subtitle. (Feel free to turn back some pages to scan and peek if you want!)

- He quenches our spiritual thirst.
- He treats us as His royal sons and daughters.
- He dwells within us and never leaves us.
- He ministers to our deepest needs.
- He reveals Himself to us personally.

- He rescues us and brings us victories.

- He reveals His transcendent love for us.

- He blesses us with genuine truth.

- He invites us to walk with Him.

- He offers us eternal life with Him.

As kingdom kids, we are rich indeed! In an 1892 sermon on Ephesians 1:3, Charles Spurgeon contrasted our priceless spiritual riches with our temporary earthly riches:

> Our thanks ought to go to God in thunders of hallelujahs for spiritual blessings. A new heart is better than a new coat. To [spiritually] feed on Christ is better than to have the best earthly food. To be an heir of God is better than being the heir of the greatest nobleman. To have God our portion [share or award] is infinitely more blessed than to own broad acres of land.[168]

Is your heart stirred to thank God with *thunders of hallelujahs* for your spiritual inheritance? Are you inspired to live for His glory in an abiding relationship? As a fruitful branch connected to the true Vine, you can enjoy unbroken communion with our awesom-azing God—by yielding to His love, trusting Him, and consenting to stay connected.[169] And your life will be a strong witness of the King of eternity, who plans to bless you spiritually for a very long time!

> Blessed be the God and Father of our Lord
> Jesus Christ, who has blessed us with every
> spiritual blessing in the heavenly places
> in Christ [because we belong to Jesus].
> (Eph. 1:3)

A poem honoring our everlasting King

IN ALL THE WORLD

All the royal births of earthy kings
> *in all the world*
>> could not compare to our Majestic King, who pre-existed before He was born in Bethlehem (John 1:1–2).

All the powerful ruling kings
> *in all the world*
>> could not compare to our Sovereign King, who reigns from an everlasting throne (Ps. 93:2).

All the royal and luxurious treasures
> *in all the world*
>> could not compare to our Matchless King, who's the incomparable gift to mankind (2 Cor. 9:15).

All the kings with glorious crowns
> *in all the world*
>> could not compare to our Conquering King, who's coming again with royal diadems (Rev. 19:12).

All the merciful and gracious lords
> *in all the world*
>> could not compare to our Crucified King, who removed our sins with His own precious blood (Rev. 1:5).

All the praises offered by royal subjects
> *in all the world*
>> could not sufficiently honor our Creator King, who deserves all glory, honor, and power forever (Rev. 4:11).[170]

WORSHIPPING GOD FOR HIS AWESOM-AZING ATTRIBUTES

He is infinite, He is ineffable, and He is/has impassibility.[171]

Dear Lord, I marvel at all Your magnificence and give You all praise and honor! Thank You, my King, for purchasing my salvation and drawing me unto Yourself, even though You are infinitely perfect and need absolutely nothing. I can only give back to You what You have given me. So I surrender my heart to You in response to Your endless love. Please help me to know You more…and love You more…and proclaim You more. I want to live for Your glory. In Jesus' name, amen.

Jesus Christ is "the Alpha and the Omega…
who is and who was and who is to come, the Almighty."
(Rev. 1:8)

"His voice [was] as the sound of many waters"
[like a mighty and majestic waterfall].
(Rev. 1:15)

*You are awesome. You're amazing. You're the awesom-azing God.
You're the fount of living water, and nothing else satisfies.*

APPENDIX A

GOD'S DIVINE ATTRIBUTES AND CHARACTERISTICS

(Based on *Systematic Theology in One Volume*, by Dr. Norman L. Geisler)

"GOD IS AN awesome God, and He should be responded to in awe," writes theologian Dr. Norman L. Geisler, author of *Systematic Theology in One Volume*.[172] Studying who God is (theology proper) leads people to marvel over His greatness and respond to Him in worshipful ways, such as David did in Psalm 139.

Since God is one indivisible Being, every attribute is true of *all* of His being. God's "attributes" are essential traits that are intrinsic to His nature (such as His holiness), whereas His "characteristics" are general traits (such as His mercy, which flows from His goodness). Although God cannot be fully expressed or *comprehended*, He can be *apprehended*[173] through His revelations to us in the Bible.

Set forth below are basic definitions of God's attributes and characteristics. For a more comprehensive treatment, see Part Three (chapters 29 to 45) of Dr. Geisler's book referenced below.

GOD'S MORAL ATTRIBUTES

- Holiness – He is totally and utterly set apart from all creation and all evil. He is pure.

- Righteousness (Justice) – He is absolutely just and right (and the ultimate standard of justice and rightness).

- Jealousy – He has holy zeal to protect His own supremacy, and He has wrath on idolatry and other sins.

- Perfection – He is infinitely perfect (morally impeccable).

- Truthfulness – He is absolutely truthful and has perfect integrity.

- Goodness (Love) – He is infinite goodness (all-lovingness) or omnibenevolent.

GOD'S NONMORAL ATTRIBUTES

- Pure Actuality – He has pure existence (without potential for nonexistence or change).

- Simplicity – He is indivisible, absolutely one (not capable of being divided).

- Aseity – He is self-existent, independent of anything else.

- Necessity – He exists necessarily (His nonexistence is impossible).

- Immutability – He is unchangeable in His nature.

- Eternality – He is timeless (beyond time).

- Impassibility – He has no needs or changing passions. (His feelings flow from His eternal and unchangeable nature.)

- Infinity – His nature is unlimited (without boundaries).

- Immateriality – He is pure Spirit (non-material).

- Immensity – He is not measurable (unlimited in extension) or nonspatial.

- Omnipotence – He is all-powerful.

- Omnipresence – He is everywhere present at once.

- Omniscience – He is all-knowing.

- Wisdom – He is all-wise (infinitely wise).

- Light – He is pure light and the Source of all spiritual illumination (the Radiant One).

- Majesty – He is unmatched in greatness, eminence, exaltation, and glory.

- Beauty – He is good and beautiful. (His goodness produces in the beholder a sense of overwhelming pleasure and delight; His beauty is reflected in creation.)

- Ineffability – His transcendent characteristics cannot be adequately expressed in human language, and He cannot be fully comprehended.

- Life – He is the living God (alive) and is the Source of all other life.

- Immortality – He possesses life intrinsically and eternally.

- Unity – He is absolutely one in essence.

- Triunity – Within His unity are three persons—the Father, Son, and Holy Spirit.

God's Characteristics

- Sovereignty – He is Lord over the universe (the King of kings).

- Transcendence – He is above all His creation.

- Immanence – His indwelling presence is in all parts of the created universe.

- Omnipresence – He is everywhere present at once.

- Mercy – He withholds deserved judgment (is merciful to the repentant). It is manifested in great compassion, and is unfailing, unchanging, and everlasting.

- Wrath – He hates sin and has righteous indignation toward all evil.

- Ineffability – His transcendent characteristics cannot be adequately expressed in human language, and He cannot be fully comprehended.

Appendix B

Apologetics Briefs

To further prepare you to give an answer "to everyone who asks you a reason for the hope that is in you" (1 Peter 3:15), we recommend apologetics briefs by Marilyn Joy Tyner, apologist. These colorful, quick-reference tools are excellent for evangelism and education.

A SAMPLE APOLOGETICS BRIEF: "WHAT SETS CHRISTIANITY APART FROM "RELIGION"?

Side A

Side B

APOLOGETICS BRIEFS DESCRIPTION

These pamphlets are high-quality study/outreach tools, which present the top evidences for the Christian faith in a nutshell. They answer those tough questions frequently posed by unbelievers. (Endorsed by Dr. John Warwick Montgomery, Brian Brodersen, Kay Arthur, and other Christian educators and leaders.)

INDIVIDUAL TITLES ARE

How Can We Know if God Exists? • Who Do You Say Jesus Christ Is? • Do All Roads Lead to God? • Why Is Bible Prophecy So Amazing? • Can a Loving God Allow Pain and Suffering? • Is the Bible the Infallible Word of God? • How Can God be Three-in-One? • Is Truth Relative or Objective? • Did Jesus Rise from the Dead? • What Sets Christianity Apart from "Religion"?

Assorted Apologetics 10-Pack
by Marilyn Joy Tyner
ISBN: 9780982916469
Retail Cost: $12.00
Full-color glossy (8½" X 16", 2 sided, gatefold)

To order these products, individually or in a combo pack, visit us online at TrueWayTracts.com.

FURTHER YOUR STUDY OF THIS BOOK

AWESOM-AZING GOD

To enhance your study on this important topic, we recommend the correlating Bible study guide.

BIBLE STUDY GUIDE

This hundred-page Bible study guide, designed for individual or group study, corresponds with the titles and attributes of God presented in *Awesom-azing God*. Through ten individual Bible studies, you will gain a clearer picture of who He is and nurture your loving friendship with Him. You will marvel at Him more…engage with Him more…then proclaim Him more. For there is absolutely none like Him (Isa. 46:9)!

Exploring Ten Titles of Our Awesom-azing God

Bible Study Guide
by Marilyn Joy Tyner
ISBN: 9781634492539
Retail cost: $8.99
Dimensions: 5" X 7"

To order this product, visit the online bookstore at TatePublishing.com or TrueWayTracts.com.

ENDNOTES

INTRODUCTION

1. Kay Arthur, "Revive Me!" women's conference held at Calvary Chapel in Vista, CA, 9/21–22, 2012.

2. Norman L. Geisler, *Systematic Theology in One Volume* (Minneapolis, MN: Bethany House, 2011), excerpts from Part Three (God), 407–408, 604.

3. Ibid., 604–612.

4. The impactful title of this book originated with my granddaughter, Kortney, who gave her dad a Father's Day card signed, "To my A-w-e-s-o-m-a-z-i-n-g Dad. I love you!" She graciously gave me permission to use her word.

THE FOUNTAIN OF LIVING WATER

5. Geisler, *Systematic Theology in One Volume*, 531.

6. Bob Hoekstra, *Day by Day by Grace: 365 Daily Devotions* (Costa Mesa, CA: Living in Christ Ministries, 2012), 105, 321.

7. Out of His infinite love, Jesus would soon go to the cross and pay the penalty for the sins of all humanity.

8. See Jer. 2:13; John 4:10–14; 7:37–39; 15:3; Eph. 5:26. See also Ps. 1:2–3; Isa. 55:1–3, 10–11; John 9:6–7; Titus 3:5.

9. Anne Graham Lotz, *Into the Word: 52 Life-Changing Bible Studies for Individuals and Groups* (Grand Rapids, MI: Zondervan, 2010), 169.

10. Mike Chaddick, Bible message on CD, "The Infinite Worth of Christ" (Phil. 3:7–15), delivered at Calvary Chapel Costa Mesa on 6/30/10.

11. Anne Graham Lotz, *Just Give Me Jesus* (Nashville, TN: Thomas Nelson, 2009), 92–93.

12. See Eccl. 3:11 and Ps. 84:2. Many people suppress their spiritual longing for God with distractions (e.g., busyness) or attempt to satisfy it with other passions (e.g., careers or relationships).

13. Ravi Zacharias, *New Birth or Rebirth? Jesus Talks with Krishna* (Colorado Springs, CO: Multnomah Books, 2008), 78.

14. Matthew Henry, "Commentary on John 7," Blue Letter Bible, 1 Mar 1996. http://www.blueletterbible.org/commentaries/comm_view.cfm?AuthorID=4&contentID=1673&commInfo=5&topic=John>

15. Chuck Smith, *Living Water: The Power of the Holy Spirit in Your Life* (Santa Ana, CA: The Word for Today, 1996), 299–300.

16. Don Stewart, *Pastor's Perspective*, call-in radio broadcasts aired on KWVE 107.9 FM, a Los Angeles station, 2008–09.

17. Christianity fulfills historic Judaism. This text box is excerpted from an apologetics brief: M. J. Tyner, "What Sets Christianity Apart from 'Religion'"? (San Juan Capistrano, CA: True-Way Tracts, 2009).

18. See Luke 11:13; Acts 1:8; Eph. 5:18.

OUR MATCHLESS KING

19. Bob Hoekstra, 105.

20. Jon Courson, *Jon Courson's Application Commentary, New Testament* (Nashville, TN: Thomas Nelson, Inc., 2003), 10.

21. See apologetics brief: M. J. Tyner, "Who Do You Say Jesus Christ Is?" (San Juan Capistrano, CA: True-Way Tracts, 2014).

22. "Jesus, the Matchless King," words and music by Marilyn Tyner and MaryEllen Walker, © 2007, used with permission of my co-composer.

23. Kay Arthur, *To Know Him by Name* (Sisters, OR: Multnomah Books, 1995), 47–48.

24. Mordecai may have been Esther's older cousin.

25. "Nothing but the Blood of Jesus," words and music by Robert Lowry (New York: Biglow & Main, 1876), public domain.

26. Josh McDowell, *The New Evidence that Demands a Verdict* (Nashville, TN: Thomas Nelson Publishers, 1999), 197–201.

27. Gary Chapman, *The Love Languages of God* (Chicago, IL: Northfield Publishing, 2002), 28–29.

28. Oswald Chambers, *My Utmost for His Highest* (Westwood, NJ: Barbour and Company, Inc., 1935 and 1963), 210.

29. Bob Botsford, pastor of Horizon Christian Fellowship in Rancho Santa Fe, CA. Los Angeles radio broadcast, KWVE 107.9 FM, "Revelation 18," aired 1/31/12.

30. *The Open Bible*, NKJV, Introduction to the book of Revelation (Nashville, TN: Thomas Nelson, Inc., 1997), 1825.

31. Josh McDowell, *The New Evidence that Demands a Verdict*, 164–192.

32. Peter W. Stoner and Dr. Robert Newman, *Science Speaks: Scientific Proof of the Accuracy of Prophecy and the Bible* (Chicago, IL: Moody Press, 1963, revised 1976), 100–110.

33. M. J. Tyner, apologetics brief "Why Is Bible Prophecy So Amazing?" (San Juan Capistrano, CA: True-Way Tracts, 2009).

34. Bob Botsford, radio broadcast, aired 1/25/11.

35. Ibid.

36. Geisler, *Systematic Theology in One Volume*, 408, 423. See description of God's "simplicity." He is a simple (indivisible) Being. Therefore, we can have all of His attention at any given time.

37. David Jeremiah, *My Heart's Desire: Living Every Moment in the Wonder of Worship* (Nashville, TN: Thomas Nelson, 2002), 26.

THE GOD WHO'S THERE

38. Elisabeth Elliot, *The Path of Loneliness: Finding Your Way through the Wilderness to God* (Grand Rapids, MI: Fleming H. Revell, 2001), 46.

39. "Forever (The Nails in Your Hands)," words and music by Richard Cimino, ©1995 Richard Cimino (admin. by Worshipsong.com), used with permission.

40. James Strong, *Strong's Exhaustive Concordance of the Bible* (Nashville, TN: Abingdon Press, 1980), Hebrew reference H3074, 62.

41. This devotional is based on the theological point of view that Christ will return before the tribulation and before the millennium.

42. Merrill C. Tenney, gen. ed., *The Zondervan Pictorial Encyclopedia of the Bible*, vol. 3 (Grand Rapids, MI: Zondervan, 1976), 428.

43. Geisler, *Systematic Theology in One Volume*, 494.

44. J. P. Moreland and Kai Nielsen, *Does God Exist?* (Amherst, NY: Prometheus Books, 1993), 289–90.

45. John Warwick Montgomery, *History and Christianity: Evidence for a Historical Jesus* (Minneapolis, MN: Bethany House Publishers, 1965), 34–43.

46. M. J. Tyner, apologetics brief "How Can We Know If God Exists?" (San Juan Capistrano, CA: True-Way Tracts, second edition, 2013.)

47. J. Vernon McGee, *Thru the Bible with J. Vernon McGee* (Nashville, NT: Thomas Nelson Publishers, 1981) vol. I, 117–119.

48. Francis Chan, *Crazy Love: Overwhelmed by a Relentless God* (Colorado Springs, CO: David C. Cook, 2008), 193.

49. Pastor Chuck Smith, *The Word for Today Bible* (Nashville, TN: Nelson Bibles, a division of Thomas Nelson Publishers, 2005), 1423.

50. David Jeremiah, 29.

51. Jon Courson, *Jon Courson's Application Commentary, Old Testament*, vol. 1, 136.

OUR DIVINE SYMPATHIZER

52. Words and music by Helen H. Lemmel. ©1922, CCLI #15960 (public domain).

53. Chuck Smith, Calvary Chapel Costa Mesa, a pastoral counseling appointment in 1982.

54. Cliffe Knechtle, *Give Me an Answer* (Downers Grove, IL: InterVarsity Press, 1986), 54.

55. M. J. Tyner, apologetics brief "How Can a Loving God Allow Pain and Suffering?" (San Juan Capistrano, CA: True-Way Tracts, 2012).

56. Bob Botsford, "The Best Is Yet to Come," aired 10/5/11. (See 1 John 3:1–2.)

57. Ibid.

58. Jon Courson, *Jon Courson's Application Commentary, Old Testament*, vol. 1, 1345–46.

59. Anne Graham Lotz, *Expecting to See Jesus* (Grand Rapids, MI: Zondervan, 2011), 179.

60. Pastor Jon Courson was Sherrie's kind counseling pastor, and Peter Courson, his son, pastored at a nearby church.

61. Sherrie Sedwick and Marilyn Tyner, testimony tract "Face to Face with a Health Crisis: Eight Lifelines to Finding Peace and Purpose through Life's Storms" (San Juan Capistrano, CA: True-Way Tracts, 2006).

62. Ibid. Sherrie's testimony tract explains how the eight lifelines applied to her own life.

63. Elisabeth Elliot, 31.

64. Ravi Zacharias, *Jesus Among Other Gods: The Absolute Claims of the Christian Message* (Nashville, TN: Word Publishing, 2000), 107.

65. See Phil. 3:10. Mary shared in Jesus' pain and rejection and experienced His intimate love.

66. Anne Graham Lotz, *Pursuing More of Jesus* (Nashville, TN: Thomas Nelson, 2009), 38.

THE LIGHT OF THE WORLD

67. Pastor Brian Brodersen, "Lights Shining in the Darkness," audio CD #BT3301, Matthew 5 Sermon on the Mount, www.Backtobasicsradio.com.

68. John Warwick Montgomery, 26–31.

69. M. J. Tyner, apologetics brief "Is the Bible the Infallible Word of God?" (San Juan Capistrano, CA: True-Way Tracts, 2012). For a classic reference book, see Neil R. Lightfoot, *How We Got the Bible* (Grand Rapids, MI: Baker Books, 1963 and 2003).

70. "Steps to Peace with God," a gospel tract (World Wide Publications, a ministry of the Billy Graham Evangelistic Association).

71. Chuck Smith, *The Word for Today Bible*, 1365.

72. M. J. Tyner, apologetics brief "How Can God Be Three-in-One?" (San Juan Capistrano, CA: True-Way Tracts, 2013).

73. Josh McDowell, *The New Evidence that Demands a Verdict*, 3–16.

74. "Walking in the Spirit: Filling" Bible study aid, *The Open Bible*, 1700.

75. Christine A. Scheller, editor, and Calvary Chapel pastors' wives, *Redeemed and Restored* (Santa Ana, CA: Calvary Chapel Publishing, 2005), 192.

76. Ibid., 187, 193.

77. Geisler, *Systematic Theology in One Volume*, 521–522.

78. Ibid., 607, 610.

OUR ROYAL REDEEMER

79. See also Rev. 13:8. Jesus was regarded as slain in the eternal plan of God, who is omniscient and outside of time.

80. M. J. Tyner, apologetics brief "Did Jesus Rise from the Dead?" (San Juan Capistrano, CA: True-Way Tracts, second edition, 2013).

81. M. J. Tyner, gospel tract "The Best Gift in the World" (San Juan Capistrano, CA: True-Way Tracts). (Available online at TrueWayTracts.com.)

82. *The Open Bible*, 1513.

83. Chuck Smith, "John 20–21," The Word for Today, Blue Letter Bible, June 1, 2005.

84. Simon Greenleaf, *The Testimony of the Evangelists: The Gospels Examined by the Rules of Evidence*, reprint of the 1874 edition (Grand Rapids, MI: Kregel Publications, 1995).

85. The expression of three days and nights probably meant parts of three natural days. Matthew Henry, "Commentary on Matthew 12," Blue Letter Bible, 1 Mar 1996. <http://www.blueletterbible.org/commentaries/comm_view.cfm?AuthorID=4&contentID=1607&commInfo=5&topic=Matthew >

86. Jon Courson, *Jon Courson's Application Commentary, New Testament,* 91.

87. Ibid.

88. One possible chronology is presented in *The Scofield Reference Bible.* See discussion by J. Vernon McGee in *Thru the Bible,* vol. IV, 495.

89. For an overview of the evidence, see apologetics brief, "Did Jesus Rise from the Dead?"

90. William Lane Craig, *The Son Rises* (Eugene, OR: Wipf and Stock Publishers, 2001), 21.

91. Chuck Smith, *The Word for Today Bible,* 1389.

92. Chuck Smith, *Faith,* 276.

93. Ibid.

94. The people also rejoiced because they gained a heart knowledge of the Scriptures (Neh. 8:12).

95. A. W. Tozer, *The Knowledge of the Holy* (New York, NY: Harper One, 1961), 60–62.

THE TREASURED TRINITY

96. "Understanding Intelligent Design" apologetics conference, sponsored by Capistrano Valley Church, San Juan Capistrano, CA, 10/26/08.

97. J. Vernon McGee, *How Can God Exist in Three Persons?* (Pasadena, CA: Thru the Bible Radio Network, 1970, revised 2005), 9.

98. For Old Testament references to God's triunity within His oneness, see "Persons of the Trinity" Bible study aid, *The Open Bible*, 1680.

99. Anne Graham Lotz, women's leadership conference "Filling Up to Overflow," held at Harvest Christian Fellowship, Riverside, CA, 4/27–28, 1993.

100. "Holy, Holy, Holy," words by John B. Dykes and music by Reginald Heber, 1826, public domain.

101. Erwin and Rebecca Lutzer, *Life-Changing Bible Verses You Should Know* (Eugene, OR: Harvest House Publishers, 2011), 169–70.

102. Dykes and Heber, "Holy, Holy, Holy."

103. See apologetics brief "How Can God Be Three-in-One?"

104. A. W. Tozer, *The Knowledge of the Holy*, 23.

105. See Rom. 3:22 and 2 Cor. 5:21.

106. See Eph. 1:4, 7, 13; 1 John 4:16.

107. This adaptation is based on a compilation of 1 John 1:1–4; 3:1; 4:13; 5:21. (See also John chapter 15.)

108. John F. MacArthur Jr., *God: Coming Face to Face with His Majesty* (Wheaton, IL: Victor Books, 1993), (quoting from the NASB), 20–21.

109. *Science Daily*, online research news publication (www.sciencedaily.com), Feb. 9, 2009.

110. *The Open Bible*, commentary on 768.

111. David Jeremiah, 53.

112. See apologetics brief "How Can God Be Three-in-One?"

113. John F. MacArthur Jr., 23.

114. J. Vernon McGee, *Thru the Bible*, vol. V, 348.

115. D. Guzik, "Text Commentaries: David Guzik (Blue Letter Bible: John)" (Blue Letter Bible, last modified 7 July 2006), http://www.blueletterbible.org/Comm/guzik_david/StudyGuide_Jhn/Jhn_17.cfm.

116. Michael Card, *Violent Grace*, 129.

THE GOD OF ALL TRUTH

117. Merrill F. Unger, *The New Unger's Bible Dictionary*, 780.

118. Chuck Smith, *Faith* (Costa Mesa, CA: The Word for Today, 2010), 83–84.

119. J. Vernon McGee, *Thru the Bible*, vol. V, 826–7 and 832–3.

120. Ibid., 841.

121. Ravi Zacharias, *New Birth or Rebirth?*, 53.

122. Chuck Smith, *The Word for Today Bible*, 1422.

123. E. L. Epstein, "Notes on *Lord of the Flies*" (a publicity release) regarding William Golding, *The Lord of the Flies* (New York: Berkley Publishing Group, 1954), 204.

124. Skip Heitzig, pastor of Calvary Chapel Albuquerque, New Mexico, "Destination: 2, 3 John and Jude," archived on www.connectiononline.org.

125. J. Vernon McGee, *Thru the Bible*, vol. V, 823–4.

126. Ibid., 829.

127. For an overview of this issue, see M. J. Tyner, apologetics brief "Is Truth Relative or Objective?" (San Juan Capistrano, CA: True-Way Tracts, 2009). See also an apologetics parable that exposes relativism, "The Metallic Gold Umbrella" (an article available as a free download at TrueWayTracts.com).

128. J. I. Packer, *Knowing God*, 20th anniversary ed. (Downers Grove, IL: InterVarsity, 1993), 19.

129. Michael Card, *Violent Grace* (quoting from the NIV), 80.

130. Chuck Smith, "Romans 14:10–13," Sermon Notes. Blue Letter Bible. 1 May 2005. <http://www.blueletterbible.org/commentaries/comm_view. cfm?AuthorID=1&contentID=5766&commInfo=26&topic=Romans&ar= Rom_14_11 >

131. See Heb.9:27. Scripture allows no possibility for people to accept Christ after their physical death. See passages where second chances to receive Christ were denied (Matt. 7:22–23; 25:11–12; Luke 16:19–31).

132. As quoted by Ravi Zacharias in *Jesus Among Other Gods*, 66.

133. Jon Courson, *Jon Courson's Application Commentary: New Testament*, 842.

OUR PRICELESS PATHWAY

134. *Pilgrim's Progress: Journey to Heaven*, a movie adaptation of John Bunyan's classic story, DRC Films, Lynchburg, VA, 2008.

135. Chuck Smith, *The Word for Today Bible*, 1368.

136. Dr. Norman L. Geisler, "Essential Doctrine Made Easy" (Torrance, CA: Rose Publishing, Inc., 2007).

137. Edward Leigh Pell, *Dwight L. Moody: His Life, His Work, His Words* (Richmond, VA: B. F. Johnson Publishing Co., 1900), 390.

138. Ibid., 391.

139. William Ray, gospel tract "Why Pray to God?" (San Juan Capistrano, CA: True-Way Tracts, 2007). (Available at TrueWayTracts.com.)

140. Illustration adapted from Dr. Norman L. Geisler, "Christianity and Culture," lecture at the Veritas Apologetics Conference held in Huntington Beach, CA, 2/19/11.

141. For an apologetic defense on this issue, see M. J. Tyner, apologetics brief "Do All Roads Lead to God?" (San Juan Capistrano, CA: True-Way Tracts, 2012).

142. *Journey to Truth: Exploring Reasons to Believe, The New Testament* (Nashville, TN: Thomas Nelson Publishers, 1993), commentary on 69.

143. Janie Alfred, speaker at women's retreat held at Calvary Chapel Conference Center, Murrieta, CA, 1998.

144. Randy Newman, *Questioning Evangelism: Engaging People's Hearts the Way Jesus Did* (Grand Rapids, MI: Kregel Publications, 2004), 85–87.

145. It is not arrogant (as some people accuse) for Christians to say that only one road leads to God. The belief that people can get to heaven by their own efforts or religious views stems from human pride (see Genesis 3).

146. Chuck Smith, "Psalm 23," The Word for Today, Blue Letter Bible, 1 June 2005. <http://www.blueletterbible.org/commentaries/comm_view.cfm?AuthorID=1&contentID=6811&commInfo=25&topic=Psalms >

147. Matthew Henry, "Commentary on Psalm 23," Blue Letter Bible, March 1, 1996. <http://www.blueletterbible.org/commentaries/comm_view.cfm?AuthorID=4&contentID=1146&commInfo=5&topic=Psalms >

148. "Christ the Lord Is Risen Today," lyrics by Charles Wesley (1707–1788), music by Lyra Davidica, 1708.

149. "New Nature" Bible study aid, *The Open Bible*, 1673.

150. Geisler, *Systematic Theology in One Volume*, 574–8.

THE EVERLASTING GOD

151. "Precious Love," words and music by Tony S. Cena, © 1993, used with permission.

152. David Guzik, "Study Guide for Revelation 1," Enduring Word, Blue Letter Bible, July 7, 2006. <http://www.blueletterbible.org/commentaries/comm_view.cfm?AuthorID=2&contentID=8103&commInfo=31&topic=Revelation&ar=Rev_1_2 >

153. *El o-lawm* is the Hebrew transliteration of "Everlasting God" (pronounced *El Olam*). James Strong, *Strong's Exhaustive Concordance of the Bible*, H5769.

154. John F. Walvoord, *Every Prophecy of the Bible* (Colorado Springs, CO: Chariot Victor, a division of Cook Communications, 1999), 7, 10.

155. Ibid.

156. Although the Quran contains some prophecy, only a few passages have alleged fulfillment, and they are vague and unverifiable. See Norman Geisler and Abdul Saleeb, *Answering Islam* (Grand Rapids, MI: Baker Books, 2002), 188, 200–201.

157. M. J. Tyner, apologetics brief "Why Is Bible Prophecy So Amazing?" (quoting prophecy scholar John F. Walvoord).

158. Jon Courson, *Jon Courson's Application Commentary, Old Testament*, vol. 1, 409.

159. In verse 5, Isaiah is referring to both the first and second comings of Christ. See J. Vernon McGee, *Thru the Bible with J. Vernon McGee*, vol. III, 285.

160. *The Open Bible*, commentary on 997.

161. Chuck Smith, *Love: The More Excellent Way* (Costa Mesa, CA: The Word for Today, 2008), 83.

162. Jesus told His disciples that He gave them prophecies so they would "believe" when the predicted events occurred (see Matt. 24:24–25; John 14:29; 16:4).

163. See John F. Walvoord, *Every Prophecy of the Bible*, 7.

164. J. Vernon McGee, *Thru the Bible*, vol. III, 923.

165. D. J. Williams, gospel tract "Where is God…and Why Won't He Help Me?" (San Juan Capistrano, CA: True-Way Tracts, 2013). ("Rupert" graduated to heaven unexpectedly on May 15, 2014, after nearly three years of homelessness. His tracts are freely distributed to homeless ministries and are available at TrueWayTracts.com.)

166. Chuck Smith, *The Word for Today Bible*, 1453.

167. Elisabeth Elliot, 178.

168. C. H. Spurgeon, "Blessing for Blessing," sermon No. 1166, delivered at the Metropolitan Tabernacle in Newington, England, on 10/26/1890 (www.spurgeon.org/sermons/2266.htm).

169. Andrew Murray, *Abide in Christ: The Joy of Being in God's Presence* (New Kensington, PA: Whitaker House, 1979), 14, 40.

170. "In All the World," a poem by Marilyn Joy Tyner, © 2014.

171. See discussion on God's impassibility, ineffability, and infinity in Norman L. Geisler, *Systematic Theology in One Volume*, 462–475, 528–530.
172. Geisler, *Systematic Theology*, 612.
173. Ibid., 528–529.